i

The Mighty Power Of Your Beliefs
by Jan L. Gault, Ph.D.

Praise for Jan Gault's new book!

❖ "Thought-provoking, insightful, genuinely helpful. I believe this book is destined to help millions."

Dr. James H. Koshi
Professor Emeritus
University of Hawaii

❖ "Gives you the ammunition to knock out self-defeating belief baggage and replace it with those mind tools leading to a richer more rewarding life."

Terry M. Roland
President
International Business Centers, Inc.

❖ "In these days of a rapidly changing and seemingly more confused world, we can either become more isolated and withdrawn, or we can step forward and face the challenges. This is where *The Mighty Power of Your Beliefs* comes in. As a surgeon, I have to make decisions and take actions daily. I know this book will help me and many others to live a more enriched life."

Dr. Yeu-Tsu Margaret Lee, M.D.
"A Woman Surgeon" Harvard

❖ "This revolutionary new book by Jan Gault helps you capture that elusive 'extra something' that can make the difference between being a runner-up and a champion. Dr. Jan makes it so easy to understand why a positive goal seeking life is the pathway to happiness and success."

James R. Sabatino
Attorney (retired Judge)

❖ "Identifies key principles shared by all successful people, and more importantly, gives you the tools for putting them into practice. Puts into reality Maslow's theory of self-actualization through developing and harnessing the power of positive thinking and positive action. Recommended for anyone who truly wants to 'live.'"

Mark A. Beede
Executive Director
United States Tennis Association
Hawaii Pacific Section

❖ "In this fast paced-get-it-done-yesterday-world, to live in quality time is your most important resource. Jan Gault is on target to help you get the most from every second…whether you want to learn how to improve your personal relationships, your financial situation, or better understand yourself, you'll find Jan Gault's new book a helpful and 'user friendly' guide."

James R. Wills
Professor & Director
Executive MBA Program
University of Hawaii
College of Business Administration

❖ "Grounded in sound psychological findings, this book shows you how to take charge of your life by taking charge of the one area where you have maximum control—your mind and its content…Positive and practical, this book is a refreshing, invigorating and inspiring blend of cognitive theory and spirituality."

Sarah D. Kuzmanoff
Past President
Hawaii Counseling Association

❖ "Can't get to Dr. Jan's seminars or classes? Learn the strategies Dr. Jan teaches at your own pace and see why her students love going to class. Packed with powerful insights, strategies and inspirations to help you make those important mind steps that lead to permanent, creative and effective living."

Shirley B. Gerum
Lecturer: Ethnobotany &
Environmental Science
Chaminade University of Honolulu

❖ "Beautifully written with exciting ideas. It's a winner!"

Barrie von Rastall-Rusch
Baroness

❖ "Substantive, powerful insights that will inspire, motivate and ignite you toward positive life changes."

Dottie Walters
President
Royal Publishing

The Mighty Power
Of Your Beliefs

Jan L. Gault Ph.D.

Ocean Manor

Cover Design by Angela Wu-Ki

Library of Congress Cataloging-in-Publication Data

Gault, Jan L., date.
    The mighty power of your beliefs / Jan L. Gault.— 1st ed.
       p. cm.
    Includes bibliographical references.
    ISBN 0-923699-25-2 (pbk.)
    1. Belief and doubt. 2. Success—Psychological aspects. I. Title.

BF773 .G38 2000
158.1—dc21   99-045577

Manufactured in the United States of America

10 9 8 7 6 5 4 3 2 1

Bulk Purchase Discounts
Books are available at quantity discounts with bulk purchase for business, educational, or sales promotional use. For information, please telephone/fax: 800-851-6114

Also by Jan Gault

Play & Grow Rich
How to Break Free From the 9-to-5 World & Profit From
What You Enjoy Most (paperback)

Free Time—Making Your Leisure Count (paperback)

Success Principles & Beliefs
(3-Tape Audio Program)

Perseverance & Passion; Strategies for Success
(CD/audio cassette tape)

25 Ways to Build Self-Esteem & Success
(CD/audio cassette tape)

The Principle of Purpose
(CD/audio cassette tape)

Vision & Courage
(CD/audio cassette tape)

**For information on scheduling Jan to speak at your
next event, or on ordering books & tapes by Jan,
please Email** info@drjan.net **or visit her web site:**

www.drjan.net

**Online Audio/Video Consultations with Dr. Jan
are currently available**

Table of Contents

Dedication

**This Book Is Dedicated to the Greatest Treasures
in My Life:
Tracy, Laura, Ken, Charles
Ian, Stephanie, Ryan, Micah, Carrie, Robin, Jennifer
Christina and Matt**
*The miracle of each of you has given me more joy and
happiness than you can ever know.*

Acknowledgments

I would like to express my appreciation to the fine people at Hawaii Pacific University, especially Chatt G. Wright, President; Nancy L. Ellis, Vice President and Dean; Dayle O. McGaha, Director; Leo M. Melanson, Satellite Campus Coordinator; and Tom Bingaman, SLDP/Satellite Program Coordinator. I also want to acknowledge Central Texas College, James R. Anderson, Chancellor; Lois A. Anderson, Dean Continental Campus; Colvin Davis, Area Director; and Maureen B. Abel, Site Director.

A very warm thank you to my psychology students for their comments and feedback on some of the book's content.

Especially I'd like to acknowledge my clients and seminar participants in Hawaii; San Francisco; Carmel, California; and throughout the world, without whom this book would not have been possible.

A big thank you to those extraordinary individuals whose work has inspired and encouraged me, including Sam Walton, Rich DeVoss, Oprah Winfrey, Jack Canfield, Dottie Walters, Dan Poynter, Shad Helmstetter, Mark Victor Hansen, Les Brown, Sterling Sills, Dr. Wayne W. Dyer, Og Mandino, Richard Carlson, Guy Finley, Dr. Lee Jampolsky, John Roger, Peter McWilliams, Dr. Willis Harman and Denis Waitley. Computer giants Edward Roberts, William Henry Gates III, and Paul Gardner Allen, whose work has saved me countless hours as a writer and educator.

A special acknowledgment and mahalo to a few terrific people whose acts of kindness cheered and encouraged me: Fred Carangan; Alexander Shor; Barrie von Rastall-Rusch; Mary Ann Gertz; Jan Marchant; and Mary Curley.

A friendly tribute to those family members for their moral support and encouragement: my mother; sisters Linda, Marilyn; and brother Richard.

Finally, I'd like to acknowledge you the reader and encourage you in your journey toward self-improvement, understanding and greater success.

Responsibility for any errors or other shortcomings in the book is mine alone.

Foreword by Dottie Walters

In this wonderful new book, Jan Gault, Ph.D. reminds me of the comments of Dr. Norman Vincent Peale who often referred to William James as the father of American psychological science. James said, "The greatest discovery of my generation is that human beings can alter their lives by altering their attitudes of mind."

Dr. Gault shows us in simple, understandable terms that what we conceive in our minds, good or bad, is what will transpire in our lives.

I have found many of Dr. Gault's quotations and ideas so full of power, I have put them up near my computer along with my other friends of the mind: Benjamin Franklin, Dr. Albert Einstein and Helen Keller. You will find this book filled to the brim and overflowing with inspiration and encouragement. In reading it I believe you will smile and nod, and say to yourself, "Yes! I know that!" so that every page will enforce your progress toward your goals.

Having begun my business career with no college, no car, a borrowed typewriter, no training except for my high school Journalism class, I deeply understand the power of mighty ideas. Holes in the soles of your shoes do not matter. What matters is putting cardboard into them. Pushing two babies in a rickety stroller with a wheel that kept falling off does not matter. What matters is using the heel of your shoe to hammer it back on. You succeed or fail depending on your ability to visualize the possible, not the impossible.

Inspiration and help await you in the pages of this precious book. I know that it will inspire you as it has me.

Dottie Walters, CSP
International Speaker, Author, Consultant
President Walters International Speakers Bureau
Publisher/Editor *Sharing Ideas Newsmagazine*
Founder of the Speakers Bureau Association,
    The International Group of Agents & Bureaus, IGAB

Preface

Why Beliefs?

Beliefs are our most vital and unrecognized resource for changing both ourselves and the course of events. Our behavior is governed by a multitude of factors—biogenetics, predispositions to act in certain ways, individual habit patterns and prevailing social and cultural dynamics—but it is our beliefs and dominant thoughts that lie at the end of the chain of causal factors influencing our lives. It is here that we have the personal power to take charge of our mental makeup and improve our lives.

While our genetic programming, predispositions and long-entrenched habit patterns are resistant to change, with the appropriate instruction and proper aids we can easily modify our beliefs and thoughts. Some of these changes will be minor and gradual; at other times they will be quite significant and dramatic, such as when you modify a major cluster of beliefs.

Although great thinkers and scientists throughout history have observed and reminded us of the giant potential of our thoughts and beliefs, we have long been tardy in taking steps to implement this wisdom. The psychology of the mind has always been shrouded in mystery, just as the heavenly bodies, sun, moon and stars were prior to the discoveries of science. We stand on the brink of one of the greatest frontiers of knowledge as we delve into our most private and challenging resources, beliefs.

I
THE MAP OF YOUR MIND

"To accomplish great things, we must not only act but also dream not only plan but also believe."
—Anatole France

Chapter 1

Belief Dynamics

"Change your beliefs and you change your destiny."
—Sterling W. Sill

The most important questions you can ever ask yourself pertain to your personal beliefs:

"What beliefs do you hold about yourself, other people and the events of your life?"

"What beliefs and thoughts about yourself surface when everything goes wrong or when you get rejected? When you fail at something that is very important to you?"

"What beliefs do you hold about money, work and your personal relationships?"

"Do you generally think of yourself as a winner...or as a loser?"

"Do you believe that you're capable of achieving your desires and dreams? More importantly, do you believe that you *will* realize your desires and dreams?"

Your Beliefs Have Powerful Consequences

The beliefs you hold—those firm convictions about yourself and events—have powerful consequences for every aspect of your life...from your financial success, to your career, your personal relationships, even your health and fitness.

Current research has shown that those persons who believe in themselves and have high self-esteem are less prone to ulcers, heart attacks, even colds and skin rashes. Our personal beliefs can lead us to depression, anger, acts of violence, even suicide. Over thirty one thousand people took their life last year. More than five thousand of these were under thirty, in relatively good physical health and might have had a promising future ahead of them. Somehow they had come to believe that their situation was hopeless and that things would not get any better. Our beliefs can indeed make the difference between life and death.

But beliefs can also have a positive impact, setting us on the path to happiness, productive living and prosperity. Outstanding accomplishments have been made by individuals who believed in themselves and their ideas. It has been said that one firm conviction, one belief, has more power than it takes to send a rocket to the moon.

Sterling Sills in his best selling book, *How to personally profit from the laws of success*, tells about an experiment done by the British Army on beliefs and physical strength. It was hypothesized that there was a strong relationship between a person's beliefs and their performance.

To check out its theory, the Army took several men and measured the strength of each with a gripping device operated by one hand. The average grip of each of the men was tested to be normally one hundred pounds. They were then put under hypnosis by the experimenter and made to believe that they were very weak. Again tested with the device, their greatest effort registered only thirty-nine pounds. Using hypnosis again, they were made to believe that they were very strong. This time when they were tested, the average grip rose to one hundred and forty-two pounds.

When they believed in themselves, they were almost three hundred percent stronger than when they believed they were weak.

Beliefs About Yourself Matter More Than What Others Think About You

What others think and believe about us is of far less importance than the beliefs we hold about ourselves.

Mohammed Ali, long before others saw him as a number one prizefighter, saw himself that way. He believed in himself and his dreams. In an interview when he was still the underdog, he declared to a reporter, "I'm the Greatest." He was convinced that he was a champion, long before it became a reality.

Christopher Columbus, Louis Pasteur and Albert Einstein in their early careers were laughed at, taunted and mocked by both their peers and the public.

Abraham Lincoln grew up in poverty and as a young boy was ridiculed and teased about his appearance and speech. He even had to borrow money for a train ticket to get to Washington and give his inaugural address.

Overcoming Obstacles and Hardships

Why are some people able to persevere until they complete their goals in spite of tough obstacles, hardship and all kinds of problems?

History is filled with examples of those who overcame obstacles, disabilities and hardships. Beethoven, the great music composer was born deaf. Franklin D. Roosevelt was bound by a wheelchair.

Martin Luther King, Jr. had a dream, a vision and a mighty belief in his ability to make a difference. In spite of the many humiliations, failures and hardships he suffered, his powerful beliefs and nonviolent methods changed the course of history. He strongly believed in the black community, humanity and the possibilities for change.

Mother Teresa lived with poverty, disease and few comforts, but she was determined to make a difference in the lives of many people. She believed in herself and in the people she was helping.

These remarkable people are no different from you or me. Each of us has the inner power to achieve success in our area of interest. Practically every week we hear news accounts of just ordinary people like you and me who have fulfilled their dreams in spite of serious setbacks, hardships and financial difficulties.

A shy sensitive girl called Jerri grew up in poverty in a rural area of the Midwest. She lived in a two-room log cabin with her mother, dad and younger sister. A pot-belly wood stove was their only source of heat during the brutally cold winters. Though her dad was a kind, honest and hardworking man, he earned barely enough to put food on the table. Jerri wore dresses made by her mother out of flowered chicken sacks. There was no money to spare for Christmas presents or extracurricular school activities.

But Jerri was fortunate. She had parents who instilled in her the belief that she could be anything she wanted to be when she grew up. Though her family was as poor as church mice, Jerri never *felt* poor.

She had a deep curiosity and compassion for people. She hated to see anyone suffer. Jerri wanted to become a psychologist and make a difference in the world. She loved going to the library and reading books about how the mind works. Even at the tender age of nine, Jerri started dreaming about becoming a psychologist and writing books to help people. Although she never had the economic and educational advantages many of us take for granted, and experienced some serious setbacks as an adult, she never lost her belief in herself and her dream. Today Jerri is a psychologist and best-selling author whose books are inspiring and helping people all over the world.

A beautiful baby girl named Susan was born with no hands and suffered many painful experiences and teasings as a child. Her dream to become a television news anchor was scoffed at by her friends. She was advised to go into a field where she wouldn't be in front of the public. Who wanted to look at someone without any hands? But Susan held on to her vision. Today she is a very happy and successful television news anchor.

Brad was laid off from work after fifteen years of service and had to file chapter seven bankruptcy. He lost his home, his car and everything he had worked and saved for. Yet he didn't give up. He rolled up his shirtsleeves and got busy turning his life around.

How do these people do it? So many of us, even with all the advantages, barely squeak by with little or only average success, far less than we're capable of achieving. What is the common denominator of these success stories? Is there a deciding factor that makes the difference?

An Unwavering Belief in Yourself

The critical factor, without exception, is that every highly successful person has had an unwavering belief in themself and what they were doing. They did not let circumstances, problems, setbacks or unpredictable conditions get in the way. Nor did they let what others thought or said get them down or deter them from their goals and dreams.

If you do not have a strong belief in yourself and your capabilities you become vulnerable to all the temptations and distractions that act to throw you off course. If you are not convinced that your goals have value or will result in some kind of benefit, you are unlikely to have the driving power to sustain you when things go wrong.

Attempting to achieve success without a solid foundation of personal beliefs is like trying to swim without water—it simply can't be done.

When you have an unwavering belief in yourself something magic happens in your life. You can accomplish the seemingly impossible, whether that is improving your career, attracting the right sweetheart or even making a million dollars.

Your beliefs have the power to shape your fate, to actually create reality and what happens to you. While a multitude of factors affect us as we navigate through life, nothing compares with the inner power of our personal beliefs.

Beliefs Versus Opinions

Our beliefs are the lens through which we see the world. They are what we hold to be true or a fact. A belief is a deep, solid conviction that something is so. It is what we feel in our gut. Often we have a lot of emotion tied to our beliefs.

Beliefs are stronger than opinions and pack a greater wallop for our life. They are more resistant to change than our opinions, and closely tied to our identity and feelings of self-worth. Beliefs often lie below the surface of our awareness, and subconsciously affect our actions.

Beliefs Come in Clusters with Negative or Positive Thoughts

Beliefs come in clusters and have an array of positive or negative thoughts attached to them. For example, some of us believe that life is a struggle, a dog-eat-dog world, and that the workday is something to mainly get through so we can get on to more important things...like watching television or going to happy hour. Many of us believe that the conditions of our life largely control our fate—whether we're in the right place at the right time, whether we get that lucky break, who we know and what opportunities happen to come our way.

Others believe that they are in charge of their destiny and can significantly influence the course of events. If no opportunities exist, they create them. They adhere to the philosophy, "If it's to be, it's up to me." Life is viewed as an adventure and a challenge, packed with new possibilities. Who do you suppose is the happiest and most successful?

Your Self-Concept

Some of the most important beliefs you have are those you hold about yourself, that make up your self-concept and feelings of self worth. For example, do you generally think of yourself as a high achiever or a low achiever? As someone who procrastinates and can't seem to complete anything? As someone who's too fat, too tall, too short, too old, socially inept or unattractive? Do you hate your body, your looks, your accent? What beliefs about yourself surface when you attempt to stop smoking, eating or drinking too much and quickly succumb to your addiction? As someone who is weak and has no will power?

There is a story about a farmer who planted pumpkins on his farm. One year for no particular reason he took a small pumpkin on a vine and put it into a glass jar. At the time of harvest the pumpkin had grown to the exact size and shape of the jar containing it. Just as the pumpkin could not grow beyond the boundaries restricting it, as humans we cannot grow and perform beyond the boundaries of our self-concept—the sum of beliefs that we hold about ourselves.

What thoughts and beliefs have you accumulated over the years about yourself and life? It's been estimated by researchers that each of us has some fifty thousand thoughts per day, and that the majority of them—over two-thirds, are negative and self-defeating. Do you think it might make a difference if you could turn some of these thoughts around? Maybe even a third of them? You bet!

How Your Beliefs Originate

How do our beliefs originate? Why do we have all these negative, self-deveating beliefs?

We inherit beliefs from our culture, our family, our social and psychological conditioning, the mass media and the many experiences that we've had.

We are not born with beliefs about anything. They have all developed in the course of living. We were born without any thoughts or beliefs about ourselves or anyone else.

We begin forming our beliefs at a very early age, long before we have many experiences or have sharpened our reasoning powers. We start logging in personal beliefs about ourselves, others and the world as early as two years of age from parents, babysitters, siblings, relatives, and television. And far too many of these early formative beliefs are based on myths, misconceptions, and sometimes just pure fiction.

The result? We wind up with a battery of half-truths and faulty ideas not only about others (such as the misconceptions we hold about many cultures and ethnic groups) but about ourselves and our own capabilities.

Unfortunately, in our early formative years, we have not yet developed the mind tools to deflect or deal with damaging input from others. If someone tells a young child they're dumb, stupid or will never amount to anything, he's likely to take it as gospel.

Resistance to Change

You might think we would learn better as we grow older, and certainly we can. However, an increasing number of psychological studies conclude that once we have formed a belief or set of beliefs, they are resistant to change, whether those beliefs are about ourselves, others, or life in general— even in the face of strong evidence to the contrary. We see life through the lens of our current belief systems and build on them to form new beliefs. Without conscious intervention, the subconscious mind automatically acts to ignore and screen out any information that contradicts our deeply-held convictions.

A story is told about how monkeys are trapped in India. A box of nuts with an opening in the top is put out by the monkey hunters. The opening is just large enough for the monkey to slide its hand through. The monkey sticks his hand inside the opening, grabs the nuts and attempts to pull his hand out. But now his hand is a fist full of nuts and the opening in the box is too small for the fist to get out.

So the monkey has a choice. He can either let go of the nuts and be free, or hang on to them and get caught. Guess what the monkeys do? They hang on to the nuts and get caught. Now we're certainly not monkeys, nor do I believe our ancestry is from monkeys, but sometimes we're not much wiser. We all hang on to some nuts that prevent us from achieving our goals. These are flawed beliefs like "I'm not smart enough." "I don't have enough time." "The economy's bad." "There are no opportunities." "I don't have any contacts." As a result, we stay stuck in a box and go nowhere.

Successful persons have a different set of beliefs: "If there are no opportunities I'll make them." "I'll find the funding I need." "I'll develop the skills that are required." "I'll learn whatever I need to know to achieve my important goals." "I'll make whatever contacts I need."

Your Giant Potential

Most of the students and clients I see have no idea what they're capable of accomplishing because they're focusing on where they are now or what they've done in the past, instead of where they could be in the future. They're burdened with a host of constricting beliefs about themselves that stunt their mental and emotional growth, their happiness and success.

If I were able to peer into your mind and observe your dominant beliefs and thinking habits, it would be fairly easy to predict your chances for success.

In the pages that follow we take a penetrating look at beliefs, identifying those that are favorably or unfavorably impacting your life. We will examine a series of powerful success beliefs and show you how to make them a part of your thinking. At the same time, you will learn how to let go of limiting, crippling beliefs.

You will also be shown how to use a number of hidden mind resources. Far too many of us have gotten into the habit of falling back on crude mind tools in our social and business dealings. It is like using a hammer and saw to operate on our brain, rather than taking advantage of the refined instruments that are available.

When you learn how to take charge of these powerful mind tools your life will change dramatically.

Chapter 1
Key Ideas

1. Your dominant thoughts and beliefs are the key determinants of your experiences and success in life.

2. Your beliefs are the lens through which you see the world, what you hold to be true or fact. Beliefs are much stronger than opinions and pack a greater wallop for our lives.

3. Your beliefs shape every aspect of your life, from your financial success, to your career, your personal relationships, even your health and fitness.

4. Some of the most important beliefs you have are those that make up your self-concept and feelings of self-worth.

5. Our beliefs originate from our culture, family, the mass media and social/psychological conditioning. Many of our beliefs are based on myths and misconceptions.

6. Without conscious intervention, beliefs are resistant to change, even in the face of strong evidence to the contrary.

7. Learning to let go of limiting, self-defeating beliefs and replacing them with empowering success beliefs will change your life.

"Become the master of your beliefs and thoughts and you will become the master of your fate."
—Author

Chapter 2

How Your Beliefs Are Shaped

"We see the world not as it is but as we are."
—**Author Unknown**

Our beliefs are shaped by a host of factors. Understanding how various forces act to influence us will help you to revise and delete stubborn beliefs that obstruct your self-improvement and stand between you and success. We'll look at eight of these.

Credibility of the Source of Information
The perceived credibility of the source of information generally has an important bearing on our receptiveness to it. Most of us give more weight to opinions stated in a prestigious journal, by an expert or a celebrity than by a street person or criminal. We continually accept, reject, and qualify the barrage of daily information to which we find ourselves exposed. Television endorsements of products by celebrities provide credibility in many people's eyes. A tattered homeless person endorsing soap is something we're unlikely to see on today's television commercials. Yet celebrity pronouncements say little about a product's value.

Whether we hold people in high or low regard, and respect or disrespect, colors our acceptance of their ideas. Politicians and attorneys know well the advantage of undermining their opponent's reputation. If doubt is cast on a person's character through negative labeling and other means, we may question the truth of anything he or she has to say.

Many of us resort to similar one-upmanship tactics in our interpersonal relationships. Discrediting others by using disparaging labels, negative body language, tone of voice and other means can give the ego a sense of superiority and power. Most everyone is guilty of this behavior from time to time. Often it has simply become a careless, nonthinking habit rather than intentional viciousness. For others, this style of communication has become an acceptable standard.

We believe if we denigrate others, find fault or some flaw in their personality to make them appear "less than," we can feel better about ourselves. Our society's on-going obsession with celebrity bashing and digging up past indiscretions is a typical example. The basic problem is our own deep-seated loss of self-worth, and feelings of helplessness in modern society, a situation that is having serious repercussions throughout the world.

A Stranger's Opinion
Interestingly, some studies have shown that a stranger's opinion frequently carries more weight with us than that of a close family member or friend. Apparently the cliche "familiarity breeds contempt" holds true in many instances. It is not unusual for children to disregard and discount most everything their parents say. Either source can be misinformed and mistaken.

The Halo Effect
Whether the information is presented under desirable or undesirable circumstances affects our acceptance of it. For

example, advertisers have long been known to make the association between their product and pleasant surroundings. We see beer commercials in a congenial bar setting with everyone smiling and having fun, and soap commercials with glorious waterfalls and bright sunshine.

Although we would like to think otherwise, these extraneous factors are impacting our beliefs and choices. Corporate giants continue to spend millions of dollars annually on such influential advertisements because of the high paying return.

Massive Evidence

In some instances, former beliefs are replaced simply by massive evidence to the contrary, such as our ideas about the shape of the earth being round rather than flat. While public consensus generally results from overwhelming scientific evidence, for a major portion of our "facts," the opposite is true. Our storehouse of facts and beliefs comes to us from the body of knowledge to which we've individually been exposed: our educational background, the books, magazines and newspapers we read, television programs we watch, lectures we attend, and so on. Thus we all wind up with diverse ideas about what's right and wrong, good or bad, and fact or fiction based on our special circumstances.

Our Experiences and Perceptions

It has been well documented that a group of persons observing similar conditions will arrive at different interpretations. We all view our worlds from the window of previous experiences, beliefs and unique perceptions. And our perceptions are easily distorted without the appropriate past experiences. An ice cube floating in a cup of water could be identified as a square of glass to someone from a tropical culture unfamiliar with refrigerators and ice cubes. Telephone poles look smaller off in the distance, it is our experience that lets us know they are the same size as the larger appearing ones close by.

Children growing up in poverty perceive coins as being bigger than do children of affluence. The full moon appears larger to our perceptions under some circumstances even though it has not changed size. Our subjective world of facts and reality varies in accordance with our previous learning and perceptions.

Some time ago when I spoke before an American Management Association convention at the San Francisco Fairmont Hotel, a physician in a meeting room adjacent to mine was addressing a group of alcoholics. The doctor placed two containers on the table in front of him: One was filled with pure distilled water and the other with pure alcohol. He wanted to demonstrate how harmful alcohol can be to your health. He pulled a big, live, wiggly earthworm out of a bag and put it into the container of distilled water. The earthworm swam around happily and came up to the top.

The doctor then pulled out another big, live earthworm and put it into the container of pure alcohol. The earthworm immediately disintegrated in front of everyone's eyes. He wanted to prove that this was what alcohol does to the insides of our body.

The doctor smiled confidently assured he'd made his point and asked the group of alcoholics what the moral to this demonstration was. A person in the back of the room said, "If you drink alcohol you won't have worms in your stomach."

We see things the way we want to see them. We often believe what we want to believe even when it's detrimental to our health and well-being.

The Need to Know
The need to know and to understand is one of our most basic motivations. Children begin asking, "Why?" as soon as

they begin talking. And no matter how scant our information might be, we tend to fill in the gaps and attempt to come up with plausible explanations. Young children, when asked why they did something, will make up stories. When people have been hypnotized by a stage hypnotist and have engaged in amusing activities, they will invent a story when confronted with their actions later, so that their behavior will seem plausible.

In other words, where there is no apparent meaning, we create meaning. We fabricate meaning. We tell stories. We need to know and we fill in the missing information to come up with explanations. We want life to make sense. And we line up our information bits to the best of our ability so our stories ring true. Psychological studies show that if we are given a problem to solve along with six pieces of misinformation, we will come up with a solution—even if we *know* the information we're given is false.

By becoming more aware of how we put together information to form our beliefs, we can move to a more sophisticated and useful way of thinking about the "missing information." Whether we are forming ideas and beliefs about ourselves, others or the world surrounding us, our information is always incomplete. And as we shall see, how we handle this very critical element of incompleteness has an important bearing on both our personal and collective well-being.

General Consensus

We tend to expose ourselves selectively to those information sources, organizations and people who share our beliefs. Conservative Republicans read magazines and hold membership in organizations that have similar views. Liberal Democrats associate with those of like mind. Many of our beliefs are confirmed in our interactions with others, by general consensus.

All of this exposure tends to reinforce our own belief systems, our own rightness about what is true and what is false. As we grow older and our belief structures become more stable and reinforced, without conscious intervention change becomes less likely. The longer a belief has been hanging around in our mind, the more we tend to regard it as an absolute and real. It has become part of our identity and how we think about ourselves.

What's Fashionable

In certain circles, some beliefs are deemed more fashionable than others. Putting these "fashions" on can give us a means of acceptance within a group. Our beliefs are heavily influenced by the groups and persons with whom we associate and seek approval. Throughout history and in different societies, various beliefs have fallen in and out of favor. Even the weight of compelling evidence to the contrary may fail to persuade us or counteract what has become popular thinking practices within the social groups to which we hold allegiance.

A Diversity of Beliefs

We live in a world of different cultures and subcultures, all holding varying sets of values, beliefs and opinions. What is astonishing is how we tend to look upon our own particular set of beliefs and opinions as right and everyone elses as wrong, in error, or, at best, only partially true. Whether they are ideological, religious, political or other kinds of beliefs, strong emotions often rise when we are confronted with opposing ideas. Individual and global wars continue to be fought over belief clashes. Both past history and present-day events attest to the destructive consequences of our antiquated and inadequate belief patterns. We have witnessed hate crimes, acts of destruction, genocide and mass suicides based on the power of destructive beliefs.

On the positive side, we have witnessed extraordinary humanitarian acts of love, kindness and compassion based on the power of constructive beliefs.

Beliefs as Your Reality

Your beliefs are your truths, what you accept as a fact, as correct. For example, "The world is round." I am a bright person." "I am not a morning person." Others get all the breaks." "Life is a jungle." "The world is going to pot." "Some people are just lucky." It is from this whole hodge-podge of thoughts, impressions, ill-formed or well-formulated beliefs that you perceive the world and respond to life in general.

In the pages that follow we'll be focusing on the content of your mind of beliefs, more so than the structure. We'll also look at the intensity or strength of your beliefs. How important are they to you and how might we break the self's bonds to limiting beliefs? Learning to stand free from your current body of beliefs and view them in a new light, as pliant moldings that can be changed according to the consequences they have for your life, is the task at hand.

The most important realization you can make about yourself is that your mind's content is not the real you. Your beliefs and thinking processes are simply mental tools that are at your disposal, to put to good use—or misuse. Throughout history, these powerful mind mechanisms have fallen into misuse largely out of ignorance and misunderstandings about their nature. We have not fully grasped how they function and shape our lives and world. We have confused who we are with an inner faculty which can be brought under our control.

The operative question is, "What kinds of beliefs are held by those whose lives are predominantly happy, productive, prosperous and creative?" Or, in contrast, "What kinds of beliefs and thoughts are governing the lives of those persons who continually struggle, who are frustrated, unhappy and unproductive?"

Your Sphere of Choice

If a head full of limiting beliefs is preventing us from realizing a greater potential, as I am suggesting, what is the solution? Can we perform mental surgery, simply go in and dissect those beliefs that are dysfunctional and replace them with healthy ones? How does constructive cognitive change occur? What is your role and degree of choice for this change to take place? Is it merely a matter of gaining insight into the workings of your mind?

Each of us has a sphere of choice that engulfs our mind of beliefs and thoughts. It is this choice realm that is at the heart of your freedom. Here and only here do you have the freedom to change, redirect or circumvent a previous response pattern. Your sphere of choice is the conscious part of you. Everyone has this freedom of choice, however slight or rusty it might be from lack of use. This is something you are born with, and it is the source of your greatest strength. As you learn to live more within this conscious sphere of being, it expands to give you greater leeway in the direction your life takes. You become the builder of your fate rather than being at the mercy of unwanted circumstances and conditions.

Cultivating this conscious sphere and working with you to dispel and defuse those beliefs that thwart a prosperous, joyful life is one of the aims of this book. You can be the person you were intended to be, eagerly awakening each day to enjoy and embrace the full measure of life's abundant riches and delights.

Chapter 2
Key Ideas

1. Our beliefs are formed and shaped throughout our life by a host of factors. Understanding this process will help you to release stubborn self-defeating beliefs that limit your success.

2. Beliefs compose our world of reality and are the lens through which we perceive our experiences, other people, ourselves and life in general. They are the basis for our decisions, choices and actions.

3. Each of us has a choice sphere that surrounds our beliefs and thoughts. It is here that you have the power to take charge of your mind's makeup and thereby your destiny.

4. When you change your beliefs, you change your life.

"The ancestor to every action is a thought."
—Ralph Waldo Emerson

Chapter 3

Your Belief Checklist

"What a man believes may be ascertained, not from his creed, but from the assumptions on which he habitually acts."
—George Bernard Shaw

If indeed you have the power to choose your beliefs and change your life, which ones shall you select?   Do you just reach into a grab bag among a potpourri of positive beliefs and pull some out? Is it that simple? By what standards do you select these invisible wonders that can change the course of your life?

The selection process hinges on a number of different criteria. Suppose you'd like to wake up each morning feeling energetic, glorious and inspired in spite of any problems facing you. Is this possible? Our feeling state seems to be so closely tied to the circumstances of our life. When things are going well, we feel happy and relaxed. Then life throws us a curve: we lose money on the stock market; our sweetheart deserts us; we discover we have a tumor. What kind of beliefs would support this "feeling good" state of mind in the face of these unwelcome events?

Perhaps you'd like to have the perseverance to get more things done, to finally complete those important goals and tasks you've laid out for yourself but never gotten around to doing. You know all the reasons and excuses for not accomplishing as much as you're capable of, yet these justifications aren't moving you any closer to completion. Are there beliefs potent enough to rescue you from procrastination and unfulfilled dreams?

Also, it surely would be nice to have a better relationship with your spouse and children. Or maybe you'd just like to *have* a spouse and some children. Most likely, you prefer prosperity over poverty, good health over illness and harmony over strife. What is the influence of your belief patterns on these desires?

Besides your own personal needs and wishes, you probably have concerns about more than one social issue: violence and crime, school safety, quality education, government debt, the ozone layer and animal rights.

Your Beliefs Make a Difference

Can the beliefs you hold really make a difference in all these areas of life? Yes, they definitely can and do.

As we said earlier, our beliefs have evolved over the years in a more or less random fashion beginning from early childhood. If as a child we were told that we were stupid or bad, we hadn't developed the mind tools to deflect this negative opinion about ourselves. On the other hand, if we were led to believe at an early age that we were superior to certain people, we did not yet have the reasoning powers to evaluate this idea. If your kindergarten teacher or classmates ridiculed your attempts to recite a poem in class, you may have seen yourself as someone who couldn't do anything right. Most of our current beliefs about ourselves, others and life in general have grown out of those rudimentary beginnings.

As we grew older, gained more information and experiences, we questioned many of our earlier impressions. And throughout our life we will hopefully continue to question and revise our storehouse of "facts." The problem is, this restructuring is largely occurring randomly and subconsciously. Instead of consciously directing the process for our overall benefit, we let the chips fall where they may. It is like building a sculpture without first having a plan and knowing what we want to create.

I am attempting to take these elusive thought constructs out of the darkness of your subconscious and bring them up for inspection under your conscious scrutiny. The idea is to upgrade your mental tools and provide yourself with the consequences you want out of life rather than falling victim to faulty thought patterns and their negative by-products.

Our first step is to identify exactly what criteria upon which to build your belief repertoire. That is, what do you want to get out of your beliefs? We know different personal beliefs produce different outcomes. But before we can decide which combinations of beliefs are best—which are the most promising mind materials—we need to decide on what we want from them. I have categorized a few of these below for which we find consensus among the majority of persons.

Checking Up on Your Beliefs

In scrutinizing your beliefs, here is a checklist of questions to ask yourself about them.

Is It on Purpose?

Does this belief keep me on target, on the path of my purpose, living my heart's desire and fulfilling my dreams?

Is It Goal Supportive?

Will it aid in the development of worthwhile goals—those goals that are right for me?

Does it facilitate goal achievement?

Does it give me the momentum to consistently follow through on important goals?

Is it fully goal-supportive?

Does It Promote Constructive Emotions?

Will it increase my joy in living?

Is it giving me the energy and enthusiasm for the tasks of life?

Is this belief conducive to the tender emotions of caring, compassion and kindness over the harsh emotions of anger, resentment and hatred?

Does It Support Social and Educational Ideals?

Will it advance goodwill and peace among all the members of society?

Will it result in better communication and understanding?

Is it conducive to the resolution of tough issues such as prejudice, racism, poverty, crime and disease?

Does It Benefit Planet Earth?

Are my beliefs in harmony with nature?

Will this belief be overall beneficial for each life form on our earth?

The Selection Process

Rather than drudging through all the beliefs you've acquired over the years and putting them to the test of this checklist, I'd like you to simply consider the above questions as your beliefs surface throughout the day. For example, if the belief, "I'm a procrastinator; I never complete anything," comes up, take a gentle, unbiased look at it, and ask yourself whether such a belief is advancing your goals.

I want you to get in the habit of stepping back from your beliefs and begin viewing them from the standpoint of an observer rather than as who you are. Again, your beliefs are not you. They are a way of seeing things, a mental facility, a tool devised for your use. And you have the power to select and fabricate the ones that are going to work best for you, that are going to enhance your life. *You* are the selector, the chooser and the creator. This is a critical distinction.

You are ultimately seeking a conscious reconstruction of the elements of your mind. In the course of your experiences, this is an ongoing process. This reconstruction is taking place now, except it is taking place for the most part automatically, without your direction and intervention. Consequently, it may or may not be supporting your best interests and the best interests of humanity, as the dice fall.

Values and Assumptions

The standards listed above have a number of built-in values and assumptions. It is important to clarify these to assess any disagreements between us. It is ultimately up to you to build your own mental framework of belief criteria. The point is to build it consciously rather than let it happen by default, by the winds of chance.

The assumptions I have based our standards upon are as follows:

1. We all have a primary purpose (or purposes) in life and we simply need to discover what it is and live it.

2. Having worthwhile goals and following through on them is important.

3. It is desirable to have abundant energy and enthusiasm for the tasks of life.

4. Both your own mental health and the welfare of others are best served by encouraging the constructive emotions of love, compassion and caring over negative feelings of anger, resentment and hatred.

5. Promoting better communication, understanding, peace and good will is everyone's responsibility.

6. Each person has a role to play in the resolution of social and educational issues that affect us all.

7. To the best of our ability, we need to take into account the effects of our actions on other life forms inhabiting earth and act responsibly.

This is not an exhaustive list, but it is intended as a starting point for the clarification of your own values as you begin mapping out your mind's content.

The Quality of Your Life Depends on Your Beliefs

The question that frequently comes up in seminars when we discuss these ideas is this: "Since my beliefs grow out of my experiences, how am I going to discard them and adopt new ones? And a whole new package of beliefs? Having the knowledge that they might be better for me or that I will get better results from this improved package sounds good on the surface, but is this really possible or feasible? After all, they represent how I think about myself and my world. They are what I perceive as true based on my past experiences."

And this is exactly right. Your beliefs make up your picture of reality. They represent your current world of reality. Nonetheless, many of our beliefs have entered our minds arbitrarily without full consideration and appraisal of either their truth or their merit.

The difficulty in changing your picture of reality is that when you let in new beliefs they may be inconsistent with your current ones, your experiences to date. They do not "match up." They do not fit the facts of your experiences so far, and they meet resistance. Always keep in mind that your beliefs are not you. They are simply mental constructs, and nature's way of helping us make sense out of the world. They exist to serve you rather than hinder you. This is where your sphere of choice and conscious intention comes in.

We will elaborate on how these changes take place as we go along. For now, I'd like you to remember only that we march to the beat of our beliefs. Our dominant thoughts and beliefs determine the quality of our life and the world in which we live. If you agree that there is room for improvement, and that some changes need to be made, then I urge you to keep an open window in your mind.

Chapter 3
Key Ideas

1. In deciding which beliefs to retain and include in your mind's storehouse, you want to. take into consideration the criteria and assumptions on which they rest.

2. Before dipping into a grab bag of new beliefs, you need to determine what results you desire.

3. Going through a painful and time-consuming process of drudging into your past history and childhood experiences to change your beliefs and your life is unnecessary. You need only clarify your present values and construct beliefs in accord with these standards.

4. The idea is to begin intentionally selecting those empowering beliefs that you want to occupy your mind.

"Anything you can conceive and believe, you can achieve."
—Paul Meyers

II
LOW GRADE BELIEFS

"Man is a credulous animal, and must believe something; in the absence of good grounds for belief, he will be satisfied with bad ones."
—Bertrand Russell

Chapter 4

Flawed Beliefs About Others

"Everybody thinks of changing humanity and nobody
thinks of changing himself."
—Anonymous

Most Problems Are People Problems
Building better personal and social relationships stands at the
heart of success in virtually every field of endeavor. Most
problems are people problems. Our educational institutions
provide us with little knowledge about improving our relationships with others. Our social environment today is comprised of people from all walks of life. Yet we have gained
little understanding of how to effectively relate to one another's differences. The ways in which we think and feel
about each other determine whether we have a harmonious,
empowered society or a turbulent, crime-ridden, dysfunctional society. Although we interact with others on a daily
basis, few of us have grasped the full implications our personal beliefs play in the social dynamics of this exchange.

Those areas that give us the most difficulty in our communications and dealings with others center around five important belief clusters: (1)Judging others based on our own competencies; (2)Denigrating those with lifestyle differences;

(3)Linear versus spherical thinking; (4)Differences on emotionally laden issues; and (5)Projecting our own value judgments on others.

Judging Others Based on Our Own Competencies

Many of us act on the assumption that everyone ought to have the same level of competency that we have attained. Those who have good self-management and time management skills wonder why others don't possess the same self-discipline. Hard driving Type A personalities who get things done easily and naturally cannot understand those who never seem to get off their butts. High-level achievers are impatient with those who move at a slower, more relaxed pace.

Those who have good writing and speaking skills fail to understand why others have such difficulty. Individuals who find it easy to get out of bed at 6:00 a.m. every morning are impatient and judgmental of those who sleep until noon. Those who maintain good diet and fitness habits often look with disdain on those who gorge down chocolates and rarely exercise.

If we have mustered up the willpower to eliminate a bad habit such as excessive smoking or drinking, we suddenly see ourselves as superior to persons who have been unsuccessful in their attempts.

This would include those who are critical of others who have been unable to figure out the financial dimension of their lives. In some third world countries, a weary mother holding a tiny, thin baby in her arms darts desperately in front of cars to the taxi with American tourists, begging for change to buy food for her child. As unsafe and pathetic as we may deem this to be, it is the best solution that she currently knows to feed her baby.

Nor are some of us that tolerant of persons in our society who don't follow the traditional 9-to-5 career path for earning dollars. If we are one of the fortunate few who find it easy to make money, it seems curious to us that others have such a struggle getting by.

Once we have mastered a particular dimension of our lives, we start taking it for granted and wonder why everyone else can't do the same. But what is often natural and easy for one person is not necessarily that simple for another. Some persons who speak with ease in front of a group of people are nervous and anxious in the intimacy of one-on-one contacts. With others, the reverse is true.

Most Competencies Are Learned

We would never expect someone to put on ice skates for the first time and suddenly skate proficiently. Nor would we expect someone who had never played the cello to sit down and make beautiful music. We forget that for humans, the vast majority of our skills and behaviors are learned, and mastery only comes with practice and interest. This is as true in the mental realm as it is in the physical realm. We are so quick to prejudge what we label as someone else's short-comings, forgetting the wide range of learned variations in everyone's behavior and competencies. A few of us have the advantage of growing up with good role models and are able to master certain areas of our lives more easily than the trial and error process most of us must experience.

Self-Righteous Judgments Harm Us All

Forming our beliefs and opinions about others based on where we are has serious consequences, not only for those who we are quick to judge, but for ourselves as well. A criti-cal word here and there, a glance of disapproval or contempt may appear harmless. The cumulative impact from this Grade D mode of thinking spread throughout a culture, how-ever, contributes to a host of social problems.

When an individual is continually subjected to uncaring emotions from those he or she comes in contact with, that individual begins to build a protective wall. We all have a number of defense mechanisms, which we use to keep our identity in tact. If an acceptable image of one's self is not supported by the majority culture, we will seek out those subcultures, groups and persons who validate our existence in other ways. This has led to gangs and violence among our youth, in the schools and on the streets. To act in ways that preserve the survival of the self is as strong a motivator as the drive for physical survival. Whenever a person feels their identity is threatened, he or she will do whatever is necessary to protect it.

Few of us recognize the powerful effects of our beliefs and attitudes, and how they contribute to the overall flavor of society—its stresses, successes, failures and problems. Change for the betterment of humankind can begin only within the conscious thought of each individual.

Denigrating Those with Lifestyle Differences

How we think about and label those who have lifestyles that deviate from our own way of life affects each of us. This would include all the buzz labels that trigger strong, conditioned emotions. Some examples of these labels would be homosexual, socialist, welfare recipient, homeless person, cultist, feminist, environmentalist and foreigner.

What any one of these labels connotes to you depends to a large extent on your belief system. For example, depending on your point of view and the current political climate, the concept of "socialist" may evoke a pleasant or unpleasant response. All labels are different and possess no intrinsic meaning of their own. The only meaning they can have is what we assign to them. What's critical for our understanding is how the use of these emotionally-laden labels affects us and their power to trigger our emotions.

These emotions may take the form of rage, anger, or disgust on the negative end of the scale to love and sympathy on the positive end. In certain instances, we have upgraded our labels of the same lifestyles to more positive shades of meaning. Using the label "homeless person" rather than "bum" may elicit a more sympathetic image. In other cases, they have been downgraded. When unfamiliar religious movements are referred to as "cults," images of mass suicide, incestuous practices and terrorist activities come to mind.

Labeling Others Can Incite Harmful Actions

The ability of labels to incite actions has been well documented. While labels serve a useful function in our language to pull together common features of an individual or group of people, we often lose sight of the human being behind the label. Responding automatically to a particular label such as "inferior," "bad," "cultist," directed at an individual or group, prevents our examination of the truth behind that label, whether it is misplaced, inaccurate, or only partially true and, more importantly, whether it has been used by someone for the emotional reaction it predictably carries with it. An advertiser who creates the association between the label "trust" and his aspirin product may be seen as harmless enough. The dictator who creates the association between the label "inferior" or "bad" and a particular race of people can, as we know, have disastrous consequences.

Applying negative labels to those we disapprove of or dislike will do nothing to change them. In fact, just the opposite is likely. They become even more resistant to change.

While labels and their shades of meaning may vary, the mind's general processing mechanisms are identical. When we do not have a clear understanding of how this process works, we are a prisoner of it, and unable to make the most effective choices in our interpersonal dealings.

Throughout our many years of mandatory education, we receive little or no instruction in how the mind functions to form beliefs and opinions. We know how to build rockets, complex computers and architectural mansions, but we are largely illiterate about the nature of our self. And we are even more ignorant of the powerful impact our thinking and communication has on the lives of others.

If you have formed some negative labels about those you work or associate with, make an effort to set them aside and look at the person behind the label. This goes for any belittling labels others have applied to you. You have the inner power to think anyway you choose. Strive to release those labels that elicit harmful results.

Linear Versus Spherical Thinking

In Western Society we tend to form opinions and beliefs about others from quantitative, linear thinking. We view others on a scale of "less than" and "more than," looking at the amount of money or good looks, the number of material possessions, educational degrees, talents, various commodities, or skills they possess.

The problem with this type of thinking is that it is all too easy to fall into the habit of associating more with "better than," or "superior," or "of greater value." We see presidents as superior to secretaries. We see physicians as more important than housekeepers and janitors. We rank people according to their occupations, the positions they hold in society, their educational background and the amount of material wealth they've accumulated. We form opinions based on the cars they drive, the neighborhoods they live in and the clothes they wear.

Making Comparisons

One of the major drawbacks of such thinking is comparison. We have come to view our value as a person in terms of these quantitative yardsticks. We get stuck in "better than," "worse than," "superior or inferior," "greater than or lower than" thinking on every perimeter. Traditionally in Western Society the dimensions that have carried the most weight are money, education, career position and physical appearance. We compare both ourselves and others according to these linear yardsticks.

The Boomerang Effect

A serious consequence of this type of thinking is the built-in bias. We devalue both ourselves and others when we think of people as being "less than or worse than" or "not as good as." This sort of Grade D thinking permeates our society in ways few of us comprehend, contributing to all the behaviors we abhor—rage, violence and crime. Undereducated in the role and responsibility we play in the overall life drama and how our thoughts impact others, swinging like a giant pendulum right back to us, we persist in the old ways, stuck in unproductive, toxic, boomerang belief patterns. We are all in the pot of soup together and affect the overall flavor of our culture and world whether we are consciously aware of it or not.

Typically, we think that our role of influence toward constructive change in society means to "convince, cajole, and manipulate" those other persons who are misguided with our greater wisdom and values. In other words, we believe the key, the bottom line, is to win those less fortunate, misguided souls over to our way of thinking. There is a predictable outcome of these methods, and it is not what we intended. Look around and see if this is not so in society. The harder we try using these obsolete methods, the greater our failure and the more crime, violence, lack and limitation we see.

Our society's current obsession and fascination with criminals, murderers and "bad" behavior only serves to perpetuate them. What we focus on consistently and allow to dominate our thoughts is what we're going to get. This again is an obvious and proven law of psychology and human behavior. Yet we go along our merry way, doing the same things we've always done, only more so, focusing on all the things we don't want to happen, and getting them threefold.

Unconditional Love

As naive and puritan as it may sound, the most important ingredient we have to offer others is stronger doses of unconditional love and kindness to counteract the violent momentum that has built up from our own indifference, insensitivity and lack of understanding. The Christian ethic has focused on the good-bad dichotomy: savior and sinner, the good guys and the bad guys. Those of us in responsible positions of authority perceive ourselves as the good guys, the saviors, the appointed ones to save or punish those who have gone astray. We see ourselves as "better than" and superior to those with the "bad" behaviors. Our whole attention is focused on what to do about other people's unacceptable behaviors.

The focus needs to be reversed. We need to consider: "What innocent, unexamined beliefs and behaviors might I be subconsciously emitting that are contributing to the present disturbing course of events in our society?" And "Can I reorient myself to focus on the unique differences in each person, making a conscious effort to seek out the real self, the pure self, that lies behind the conditioned behaviors?" This is what we need to be asking ourselves in our day-to-day interactions.

The more potential good we are able to see in others, the more that good will expand and blossom. As we learn to let go of our judgments, feelings of fear and reactive thoughts and actions, we come closer to building a society based on good will, trust and creative cooperative efforts.

Spherical Thinking

A step in this direction is to begin viewing others from the perspective of what has been referred to as "spherical thinking." Instead of viewing others in comparative terms on scales running from fair to good, better, best, or using either-or thought modes of the good guys and the bad guys, we need to begin thinking of others as simply different. Presidents are not better than janitors. They simply have a different set of interests and capabilities; the same is true for all people— whether they work in a factory, on the farm or play golf all day.

Each of us has a role to play toward the harmonious functioning of society. When someone's opportunities for viable self-expression are blocked or thwarted, he or she is likely to resort to activities disruptive to others. As an increasing number of individuals and organizations go out of kilter, all of society suffers.

Positive Social Change Starts with Individual Change

Positive change occurs when we recognize and define our roles in cooperative efforts rather than through separationist communications. Instead of pointing the finger of blame and arguing, "Why don't you shape up?" let us try, "How might I change my own thinking to improve our situation?" Instead of the attitude of "Why must *you* persist in all those stupid, irrational, unacceptable behaviors," examine what beliefs within yourself may be sustaining the disequilibrium.

If we take the time to listen to almost anyone, no matter how tough or bad the person appears, we will hear that all he or she wishes is to be thought well of and treated like a person, with respect and dignity. No one likes to be looked down on. Far too many of those people "out of community" or on the fringe of society find illegal means to accumulate the material symbols of success—money, cars, jewelry— simply in the hopes of validating their existence as worthwhile people and receiving better treatment.

Thinking about others through our comparative lens serves no useful purpose and denigrates the miracle of each individual's uniqueness. Once we have learned to take off the blinders of our conditioned comparison responses to other human beings, we will be amazed at the beauty to be discovered. Prejudgments, biases and low expectations for others only set the mold of their identity. Most of us never become aware of the special hidden qualities of those we have shut out with our tainted labels. It is no wonder that they run for shelter away from the fold, the community at large. All wind up as victims. We can no more escape those "bad elements" of society than we can escape a sore on our body. Unless it is attended to, it can spread and affect our overall health.

Our attitudes and beliefs are felt by those around us. We are responsible for our private thoughts as well as our actions. Building personal beliefs that generate feelings of love and caring rather than hate and condemnation go a long way toward improving the society in which we live.

Belief Clashes Over Emotionally-Laden Issues

When we find ourselves in situations with those who hold beliefs that are diametrically opposed to our own, strong emotions often prevent good communication. These beliefs may center around issues of marriage, child discipline, educational practices, politics, religion, business practices, sexual orientation, abortion, or any other issue that holds an important place in our minds.

The problem is not that people have different belief systems or that we disagree with their points of view. Theoretically, most of us adhere to the notion that everyone has a right to his or her own beliefs and standards of living insofar as these do not interfere with the rights of others. The problem lies in the either-or thinking process that frequents these belief clashes with others; one person's belief that he is "right" and the other person or group is "wrong." The consequences of this right-wrong, good-bad judgmental thinking is that we are unable to reach common-ground solutions to resolve differences and improve our practices and relationships. We see this on every level of communication, from the family to social, economic, political and religious groups.

View Others' Beliefs as Something They've Learned, Not Who They Are

As we become more adept at viewing other people's beliefs and behaviors as the best they're capable of right now, rather than wrong, bad, stupid, ignorant or all the other negative labels we attach to ideas different than our own, we position ourselves for cooperative efforts and constructive change. Our own beliefs and the opinions to which we have become so attached fall into the same class. They are there by virtue of our informational exposure, reasoning processes and experiences to date. They are no more (or no less) valid than anyone else's.

A healthy system of beliefs keeps us free from friction, disharmony, anger and other toxic emotions as we encounter others who hold ideas and opinions contrary to our own. A flexible belief system allows us to view differences as an opportunity to learn something new, though not necessarily to change our own minds. And if we so choose, we can best influence others toward change from this vantage point. As we learn to "stand back" from our belief systems and the beliefs of others, we free ourselves from attachment, bias and judgment.

Taking note of all the amazing belief differences reflected throughout the course of history lends a new perspective on our day-to-day personal interactions and our needs to validate our existence by being "right" or to prove that our beliefs are superior to anyone else's.

History's Amazing Beliefs

During the seventeenth century esteemed physicians believed illness was caused by bad blood. They used leeches and lizards to suck the blood from sick patients. Many died. In 1879 Gustave LeBon, a founder of social psychology, expressed his belief that women's brains were closer in size to those of gorillas than to the more developed male brains. During the Middle Ages over one hundred thousand persons were believed to be witches and burned at the stake.

During the Golden Age of Greek civilization, learned male scholars considered it a status symbol to have strong-minded young male lovers since women were believed to be the weaker sex. In America, as recently as the early twentieth century, women who dared enjoy sexual relations were widely believed to be trollops and whores.

Today's Beliefs Become Tomorrow's Myths

We need to keep in mind that our cultural and personal beliefs are only as good as our current level of knowledge and understanding. Today's dominant beliefs become tomorrow's myths. The idea is to keep our perspective about how beliefs change and the many ways they impact our lives.

Learning to let go of an attachment to our beliefs frees us from all the explosive emotions and separationist communication that generally go along with significant belief differences about highly-charged issues.

Projecting Our Own Value Judgments on Others

Our values, like our beliefs, are internalized from the culture in which we happen to grow up and the subcultures with which we identify. Some of these values have been examined and thereby accepted, modified, or rejected. Others lie unexamined, buried in the recesses of our mind. In a society still in the embryo stages of awakening to the sources of its habits and behaviors, most of us live out our days without the benefit of knowing exactly where we stand and why we stand on many of our values and beliefs.

In Western Society, hard work, self-discipline, having a job, providing for the family, having good relationships and using time productively are valued and have been internalized by the majority of us.

As with judging others based on our own personal competencies, we are often quick to criticize and label those who do not live up to the values we hold.

"Why can't he get a job and get off welfare? He must be lazy and no good."

"What's wrong with Marge that she can't finish anything she starts? Hasn't she got any self-discipline?"

"Why is he such a womanizer? Doesn't he have any moral values?"

"How can she believe in such ridiculous educational practices?"

"Why are they taking another vacation on their salary?"

"Look at that fat woman eating chocolates. Hasn't she got any will power?"

We are prone to project our own values on others, and to interpret their behaviors through the lens of our biases.

My purpose is not to undermine or even to question the values that you hold. In all probability, mine are pretty much the same as yours. The goal is not to throw out our values, only to deepen our appreciation of differences, and let go of the tendency to judge, condemn and criticize.

An argument could be made that as we come to fuller understandings of our nature and the world in which we live, values have evolved to preserve and enhance our lives. Still the question could be raised, "Why then are we no freer than past generations from poverty, senseless crime, suffering, ongoing wars, and all the other problems that plague humanity? Where is the humanitarian progress?"

Outmoded Thinking Habits and Beliefs Result in the Breakdown of Effective Communication and Contribute to a Host of Problems

Certainly if our ways of thinking and methods for change were working, we would see some evidence of that change throughout history. It would be reflected in our smallest social unit, the family, as well as among nations. At both levels violence has shown no decrease but would seem to have escalated. While domestic violence threatens to tear our homes apart, there is a nonstop battle of nations threatening to tear our world apart.

Practically all our interpersonal clashes go back to the basic denominator of a lack of understanding and the question "Why?" The need to understand is one of our strongest motivations. When events occur that we do not understand, we search desperately for explanations and answers. We want to understand. We want to make some sense out of man's inhumanity to man. And we want to take action that will solve our problems. But we forget that actions stem from beliefs, and if we are ever to find real solutions, we must attend to the vital link of our thoughts.

It is easy to fall prey to unviable, dead-end belief cycles in our dealings with others. Placing blame, attaching negative labels and taking retaliatory actions at an individual level are the splinters of dynamite that cumulatively turn nations against nations. We have no history without wars. We have few individuals without resentment, anger and blame. Until there is a significant increase in the number of individuals who have learned to think and live free of these destructive emotions, there can be no peace in our cities or nations free from war.

It seems such a tiny thing for a person to take charge of his or her thoughts and beliefs. Yet if you have never tried to go even a few hours without one hostile or negative thought, you are in for a rude awakening when you do. Thought mastery is our most difficult challenge, and it is our single greatest hope for better communication and living in harmony with one another.

Your Personal Success

At this point you may be asking, "What has all this got to do with my success? I just want to get out of debt and make more money. I don't have any higher purpose to improve the world."

Umm...well, actually you do. We all do. And, we can best help ourselves by helping others. When we genuinely care about others and their needs, we become more service oriented. We think in terms of producing a product or service that will benefit or in some way enrich the lives of others. We seek to improve our work, ourselves, or our business so that we all might profit.

The shortest route to success is not only to believe in yourself but to believe in others, to care about them and their desires and needs. Success with others, and for ourselves, comes when we have learned to let go of those flawed beliefs that result in poor communication, misunderstanding and ill will.

Chapter 4
Key Ideas

1. Perceiving and judging others through the lens of our own competencies, values and beliefs serves no useful purpose.

2. Linear thinking modes of comparison and quantitative yardsticks such as either—or, better than—worse than, superior—inferior, contribute to a breakdown in communication among humans and result in violence, crime and other destructive behaviors.

3. Labeling others negatively is an outmoded way of thinking with predictably undesirable consequences for all concerned.

4. Learning to take a larger view of humanity beyond judgments, comparisons and labels, we free up energy for more creative responses and endeavors.

5. Our own values, beliefs and opinions are not hard facts but have evolved from a host of factors: our unique perceptions, our inherent culture, the sum total of our experiences and education, as well as personal reflection. By recognizing this, we can more readily appreciate and accept one another's differences. Acceptance does not mean condonation, but is a spirit of mind from which cooperation and constructive change are possible.

6. Personal success comes when we believe in others and have a genuine concern for their welfare and happiness.

"Change your thoughts and you change the world."
—Norman Vincent Peale

Chapter 5

Personal Belief Deficits

"A (person) is shaped to beliefs long held however uncritically—as the roots of a tree that has grown in the crevices of a rock."
—Oliver Wendell Holmes, Jr.

The most important beliefs we hold about ourselves stem from the way we define our value as a person. This is commonly referred to as our self-worth and self-esteem. Typically, we view ourselves and how well we're doing within the framework of three broad categories which are proving to be detrimental to our mental, emotional and financial health.

Self: A Package of Commodities

Many of us see our worthiness as a function of our achievements: what we've accomplished over the years, our educational degrees, trophies, awards and recognition. We might also appraise ourselves according to various personal qualities: being considerate of others, expressing kindness, and adhering to the Golden Rule. Or we may rate ourselves in terms of material assets: our accumulation of money and the things money will buy, such as furniture, cars, homes, jewelry and collectibles.

If the measure of our worth lies in our material possessions, our products and services, the qualities of our personality, what of those who are void of achievements, good qualities and good habits? Or those who are limited in these areas? Have they no worth, or diminished worth? And where are they to find it? Only by building on successful experiences? Being told that they are innately good, a special unique person, one of a kind, a child of God?

I haven't found the average person, the intelligent person or the geniuses of human nature to provide us with very satisfactory answers. Psychologists have educated us to separate the person from the behavior, and they point out that the person, the real you, irrespective of your behaviors, has value and worth. And this is absolutely true. Few human beings, however, *feel* worthy or happy or successful in the face of a continual barrage of unwanted circumstances or an ongoing stampede of bad habit patterns over which they seem to have little control.

Pat Answers to Self-Worth Don't Work

How can you convince yourself that you are deserving if deep inside you do not feel worthy? What makes us worthy anyway? Why do some people feel okay about themselves no matter what their situation, while others continually struggle to find even a small amount of self-acceptance and confidence?

Is it possible to perceive ourselves as worthy and deserving, irrespective of how well we are doing? Can self-worth become a constant, a stable, unchanging given for us, in spite of how far we deviate from a prize package of achievements, personal habits and material assets? And what would be the consequences of such a genuine belief about ourselves?

To approach these important issues, we need to go beyond our usual pat answers and look at self beliefs within the context of a larger web of the mind's contents.

Identity Demons

Another limiting way of looking at self-worth is in terms of your identity, that is, the primary dimensions along which you see yourself.

The closer your identity and resulting self-esteem are locked into the significant dimensions of your life, the greater your vulnerability. These would include your career or job, your relationships, and your health or fitness.

How Do You See Yourself?

If you see yourself primarily in terms of the job or career position you hold, and you are fired, laid off or in transition between jobs, your self-esteem is going to be in jeopardy. This would also apply if you were not doing so well on the job and are passed up for a promotion. I see this often among my clients. One highly intelligent woman client, a certified public accountant, who worked for a large firm became victim to corporate cutbacks and found herself out of a job. After four months with no success at finding a new position, she began having serious doubts about herself and her capabilities. She had fallen into the trap of judging herself based on her career success.

On the other hand, if your major focus in life is having a good relationship and yours is less than ideal, as most relationships are, or your relationship is nonexistent, again your self-esteem plummets. If your health and fitness are below par, you have gained ten pounds, can't keep off the weight, and this is of major importance to you, once again your self-esteem suffers.

In other words, a big chunk of most people's lives is contingent on their career, financial situation, relationship and personal appearance. The vast majority of us have difficulty when just one of these important dimensions goes out of kilter. If you are going through a period when *all* of the vital dimensions of your life are falling apart, and your identity is strongly tied to them, where does that leave you? Not in the brightest of worlds.

Insecure About Who We Are

In extreme instances, we see financial losses driving persons to suicide. During the Great American Depression, large numbers of people sought an end to their existence. Their beliefs told them that without money life no longer mattered. In the breakup of a relationship, or a divorce, most people suffer mental anguish and self-recrimination. A vast majority of us continually admonish ourselves for being unable to lose weight and keep it off.

Although volumes have been written in popular magazines and self-help books telling us we're okay and to stop beating ourselves up for all those things we're unable to do perfectly, we're still very much insecure about who we are. On the one hand we're told we're okay; while right along with it is the other message to spiff our lives up—become more successful, get a better job, improve our personal appearance, have a good relationship, get unstressed and by all means, be happy.

When does our worthiness become an irrevocable pact with ourselves?

Cultural Bias

Another way of approaching the way we view ourselves and our self-worth is through the eyes of the culture and society in which we find ourselves. A culture that praises hard work will place more value on those people who work hard.

A culture that esteems education will place more value on those individuals who have earned associate, bachelors, masters, and doctoral degrees.

Our appraisal of our worth stems to a large extent from the beliefs we have inherited and internalized from our culture. If your culture values self-discipline, a good job, higher education, traditional marriage, good looks and material possessions, and you fall short in several of these areas, you're likely to pay a price. Although we tend to seek out subcultures, organizations and individuals who embody our particular lifestyle and interests, we are never free, in a full sense, from the biases and values of our dominant culture.

No matter how private our lives, we can never fully escape from the influence of our culture. We must commute to work, go to the grocer's, shop and attend social events. A look; a remark; a slight because of our appearance, race or physical disability; the car we drive; the home we live in; the way we part our hair, all play a role in the formation of our self-concept, how we perceive ourselves and our degree of self-esteem.

To get a handle on the way your culture influences your beliefs and feelings about yourself, you need to bring it up to your conscious attention in order to defuse any negative energy that is diminishing your value as a person.

Your Present Scenario Versus Your Preferred Scenario

Notice that in all of these examples, the common denominator has to do with what we have or are versus what we believe we should have, do, or be: the present scenario of your life versus your preferred scenario; your actual state of conditions versus an ideal, future state of affairs.

Some psychologists have measured self-esteem in terms of this gap between your actual state and your ideal state, that is, where you perceive yourself to be on all the significant dimensions of your life versus where you'd like to be, your preferred state of existence. This might relate to your job, cash flow, personal relationships, physical attractiveness, sex appeal, self-discipline, or any other important dimension. The greater weight a particular item carries, and the greater the gap between where you perceive yourself and where you'd prefer to be, the lower the self-esteem.

Let's say on a scale from one to ten on attractiveness, you rate yourself at the low end of the scale, a three. When asked how important this attribute is to you on the same scale, you respond with a high nine. In other words, there is a large gap between where you perceive yourself and where you'd like to be. A significant number of these large gaps in many areas of your life can seriously undermine your feelings about yourself.

A small to moderate gap between your actual state and your ideal state is considered healthy and desirable, because this can result in the energy for change toward the more ideal state and realizing more of your potential. On the other hand, too great a gap is likely to result in being frustrated, over-whelmed and possibly getting stuck, unable to take effective action and advance toward a more ideal state.

Basing Your Self-Worth on Success Contingencies Is Hazardous to Your Well Being

Most educators and psychologists offer instructions aimed at assisting their students or clients in reducing the gaps be-tween the actual states and the ideal states, thereby increasing their self-esteem. If your education, job skills, personal ap-pearance or finances are less than what you would prefer, then the idea is to improve yourself, thereby moving toward a more preferred state.

The problem with this is that as soon as you approach the preferred scenario, it recedes, creating more discrepancies between where you are and where you want to be—more riches, a better relationship, better health. Upon reaching our goal, we set a higher goal, then an even higher goal. This is all well and good, except when it becomes a standard for your value as a person, you never quite arrive. I have counseled millionaires who feel insecure and miserable, having figured out how to fill up the hours making dollars but still not managed to come to terms with their purpose and value as a human being.

And as quickly as you close the gap in one area of your life, another pops up to taunt the way you feel about yourself. You become better educated, but you still stand in the midst of a bad relationship. You take off ten pounds and move closer toward your ideal weight, then the stock market crashes; you lose a bundle of money and find your financial situation in peril. Perfection in all the important dimensions of our life never quite becomes a reality.

This is repeatedly found in my practice. No matter how much many of my clients appear to have going for them, they fall into the despair stemming from low self-esteem according to the conditions of their life. One aspect of life is always less than it could be.

If it is not in your best interests to hold beliefs that place your worthiness and value as a person at the mercy of a series of success contingencies, achievements, personal attributes, financial assets and the like, then what?

Strive for Unconditional Self-Acceptance

The key is unconditional self-acceptance.

Can you still have goals and move toward greater success in those areas you desire? Yes. The important difference lies in your motives. Your actions will no longer be to prove yourself, to prove that you are indeed capable and "worthy." You will have a fundamentally different perspective about your life in that you believe in yourself, like yourself and accept yourself—no matter what. No matter what you are able to accomplish or not accomplish. No matter how many times you make mistakes and fall on your face. No matter how many relationships disintegrate. No matter how many bad habits—smoking, drinking, eating—you happen to have. And no matter what unpleasant circumstances plop themselves in your path.

The difficult question is how do you arrive at this unconditional self-acceptance and maintain it throughout your life in spite of the bumpy roller coaster of imperfect living?

It might also be asked, "If you're not measuring yourself along the lines of what you believe you should be doing, aren't you likely to lose the driving force of trying to improve? Won't this make you laid back, unmotivated and self-satisfied?"

No, just the opposite. It will have the net effect of freeing up your energy. Your actions will no longer be instigated by false motives to make yourself feel worthy, important, or somebody. Letting go of "self-worth as a function of a string of success contingencies" frees you to discover your true interests, to know your real purpose in life, whether those are in accord with the particular culture in which you live or not. You escape from the conditioned set of success perimeters of society. You arrive at a place and stand in a position where your choices can be more independent of both cultural influence, other people's values and biases, as well as your own past history of beliefs and habits.

No Need to "Show and Tell"

When self-worth finally becomes a given (we're not there yet), then you do not need to squander time and energy indulging in activities that serve no better purpose than soliciting other people's acceptance and praise. You do not need to accumulate possessions that make a statement about your financial credibility. You do not need to "show and tell" to prove your worth to anyone, whether that proof be via educational symbols, material symbols, or people symbols of success.

In essence, you do not need to stuff your life with proofs that you are a good, worthy person by living a life of goals that may be far removed from your true purpose.

You are free to do what you want to do, what you determine is right and best, free from the biases of others, your culture and your own internal structure of conditioned mind constraints. You then have no need or fear of other people's approval or disapproval, other people's rewards or punishments, or your own self-sabotaging emotions of guilt and shame. You are free to act in your own way, in your own time, according to the dictates of your personal values and genuine interests. In other words, you become your own person.

Start Planting Belief Seeds of Self Worth

In a later chapter, you'll be given specific instructions for building powerful personal beliefs relating to self-worth. For now, to start the process, I'd like you to begin planting the seeds of unconditional self-worth with the following affirmations:

1. I have the right and choice to manufacture my own beliefs about myself and my world. I select those beliefs that have beneficial consequences.
2. In spite of my circumstances, past mistakes, lack of achievements or personal shortcomings, I choose to believe in myself and that life is worthwhile.
3. I conduct myself as well as I know how at this point in time and forget the rest.

4. When another person's appraisal or judgment of me is unkind, I make the choice to deflect their negative energy without any ill will.

5. I am more than my job, my relationships, my physical body and financial assets.

6. I do not find it necessary or wise to evaluate myself according to any cultural standards.

7. I no longer quantify my worth as a person according to the package of achievements, education, awards and material possessions I possess.

Remind yourself of these beliefs frequently. Small mind steps result in big life changes. Appreciate yourself for being the person that you are today.

Chapter 5
Key Ideas

1. It is possible and desirable to view yourself outside of a string of success contingencies, and to experience unconditional self-acceptance.

2. You can learn to perceive yourself from a position that is independent of cultural values and biases.

3. The real you is more than your ego's package of attributes, behaviors and possessions.

4. The dimensions by which we generally define ourselves such as education, career, status, appearance and relationship are not the measure of your value as a person.

5. Your deepest purpose is revealed to you as you discover how to strip away the heavy baggage of trying to prove yourself.

6. Begin planting belief seeds of self-worth. Small mind steps result in big life changes.

"The belief that becomes truth for me...is that which allows me the best use of my strength, the best means of putting my virtues into action."
—Andre Gide

Chapter 6

Faulty Belief Patterns

*"The greatest ocean cannot sink the smallest ship until
some of the water gets in."*
—**Sterling Sills**

Grade D Beliefs

All of us have hundreds if not thousands of beliefs and
opinions on a variety of topics. The beliefs we hold that
evolve around our key concerns, however, have the greatest
influence on our quality of life. For most of us in modern
society, these center around our careers, work, financial
concerns, family, relationships with others, and health and
fitness. The way we view time, the chain of events in our
life, also has important consequences for us.

In this chapter we'll look at five belief patterns that get us
into the most trouble. Faulty modes are generally evidenced
by conflict and discord rather than by the smooth rhythm and
harmony that characterizes healthy patterns.

In talking about beliefs, always keep in mind that beliefs
and thoughts, although invisible, have far-reaching effects on
our experiences, our successes or failures, our relationships
and all the important dimensions of our lives.

The belief patterns we'll examine are all interrelated and overlap one another to some extent. I have broken them down into separate segments for discussion so that you can more easily spot them in your own experiences.

Faulty Belief Pattern No. 1
Making money involves work, hardship, struggle and pain. I do not believe I can make a great deal of money from my creative interests or those things I truly enjoy.

People coming from this belief orientation are unable to make the connection between making money and their creative endeavors. They simply cannot *believe* that it is possible to do what they really want to do and like to do, AND make money at it. At a gut level, they believe that it is necessary to "*work*," that is, do something distasteful or difficult in order to make a great deal of money. They do not understand that affluence and abundance can be a natural by-product of the pursuit of their dreams. They are unconvinced of the merit of those deep stirrings inside of them that tug at their heartstrings, prompting them to take action in the direction of their own special interests.

People here typically fall into one of three groups:

A. In the first group, we find those who give up on their hopes and dreams and creative inclinations to pursue an unwanted or unsatisfying job that pays the bills.

B. A second group of people, where many of us find ourselves, is settling for a career that only partially or minimally allows us to keep our dreams alive.

C. Finally, in the third group are those who have given priority to their creative endeavors but do not believe that they'll ever be able to support themselves through their efforts here.

Which group do you fall into? Each of these belief orientations has significant consequences for your life. Let's look at some of the more specific thoughts and self-talk we feed ourselves that maintain these self-defeating patterns.

Group A
Working to pay the bills or just make money

With this group we usually find a train of thoughts and beliefs such as:

"Once I've accumulated enough money and realized financial security, *then* I'll be ready to pursue my dreams and those activities I really care about."

"What else can I do? I have to pay the bills. I don't see that I have any other choice."

"It doesn't really matter what I want to do or would like to do. I don't know that I have any creative talent anyway."

"I'll go all out to make as much money as I can as fast as I can, *then* I'll figure out the important stuff."

Self-messages like these perpetuate a bad situation. We've got it all backward. Chasing the buck, spending the bulk of our time doing unfulfilling work alien to our true interests is unlikely to bring us either riches or any future time free for "the important stuff."

Although we may still find creative outlets in our discretionary time, the vast majority of us, after a long day's work, fall back on passive leisure pastimes, such as watching television, reading the newspaper or going to happy hour at the local pub. And when we give up on those things that are important to us, our hopes and dreams, small wonder we feel a sense of listlessness and resignation. Life has lost its luster.

Group B
Career Settling

Some of the thoughts and self-talk sustaining this belief system are:

"The job I have and the work I'm doing are not so bad. I should be happy that I even have a job that pays the bills."

"There are some aspects of my work that I enjoy. It's the best I can hope for. I'm not sure what change would bring. It could be worse."

"Sure I'd like to write a book, open my own hobby shop, or live in a smog-free environment. But let's get realistic. I have to live wherever I can find a decent job. And open my own business? That's pretty risky. What if it fails and I lose everything?"

We've filled our mind with a set of rationalizations and beliefs that shut out the inner urgings of our creative self so we can keep on doing what we're doing.

Group C
Creative Hobbyists...Scraping By Financially

Persons here pay only minimal attention to profit or income, just enough to stay afloat, squeak by and cover the bills every month. Their primary focus is on their special projects with little regard for the profit potential. They tend to see themselves as survivors rather than success masters.

It is all well and good to make some financial sacrifices for a period of time while giving full attention to your creative interest. What we are referring to is not the healthy cycle of learning, productivity and then reaping the rewards of one's efforts. It is those who hold to the beliefs that "Life was meant to be difficult. That's just the way it is. It will always be a struggle to pay the bills and take care of the financial end of things." And this of course becomes a self-fulfilling prophecy.

Pervasive belief fragments found in this group are:

"I really have no idea how to earn dollars from my dream."

"Anyway, I'm a creator. I don't want to be bothered with sales and marketing, or promotion of my work. Business bores me."

"It will always be necessary to work at something else, at least part time, to pay the bills and cover my expenses."

Coming from these beliefs, you may well find your time divided, continually juggling what you really want to do with what you have to do to meet expenses. You never quite get rid of the stress of financial concerns to have the freedom and peace of mind to be as productive and successful as you otherwise might.

Personal conflicts revolving around giving expression to our creative talents while simultaneously attending to demanding financial concerns have become widespread in our society today. We see more and more popular books and public educators addressing the problem. In spite of all the helpful information that is readily available on this issue, only a few of us have been able to successfully resolve our dilemmas.

Faulty Belief Pattern No. 2
There just isn't enough time to get everything done.

This is actually true. No one person can do everything. Where such a belief gets us in trouble is when we apply it to our important goals, our hopes and dreams. I have discussed this at length in *Free Time* (Wiley & Sons, N.Y.). The main point I want to convey is that if you do not honestly believe you can finish a college course, get a degree, start a business, complete a book, make a video tape, buy a home of your own or whatever your desire, it absolutely won't happen.

We cannot do everything, but we can and will do whatever we genuinely believe is possible for us and what we have the sufficient desire to follow through on.

"Time" is also frequently used as a rationalization for avoiding (1)something we don't really want to do (low motivation); (2)the fear we may not succeed (fear of failure); (3)the fear we will indeed succeed but wind up with more responsibilities than we bargained for (fear of success); or (4)the feeling that we don't deserve to be successful (low self-esteem). These belief pitfalls are frequently buried beneath our habitual "I don't have enough time" talk.

Not having sufficient time is really a bogus reason for failing to follow through on our important goals. Almost everyone can be what they want to be, do what they want to do and achieve whatever measure of success they desire. We are fully capable of arranging our time segments into whatever shape we'd like our life and experiences to take.

Faulty Belief Pattern No. 3
No one cares what I do, so what's the point?

Sometimes those who see themselves as having been dealt a bad hand in life and subjected to more than their fair share of pain, hardship, rejection or defeat, along with little kindness, support or understanding from others, may succumb to the untenable thought position that "no one cares about me, so why should I care?" Such a stance can lead to giving up on oneself, deciding it is pointless to attempt following through on one's goals, and giving up on life in general, doing only what is necessary to get by.

Our prisons, youth rehabilitation facilities, mental health clinics and streets housing the homeless are overflowing with those who have lost hope in themselves and others. We talk a lot about love and caring in our society, yet teachers, psychologists, policemen, physicians, nurses and others in the helping professions are all licensed to fulfill their duties with nil instruction in the caring emotions of kindness, appreciation, trust, respect, acceptance and unconditional love.

Ultimately, however, the burden lies with each individual. Those who are in need of receiving the caring emotions the most, we find, care the least about others, not having learned that the best way to gain something in one's life is to give it away first. Life gives back to us in direct proportion to what we give to life.

If you feel no one cares, and we all go through periods where we feel unloved and unappreciated, the best remedy is to revamp your own view of others. While you may have little control over what others feel or say or do, you can always take charge of your own mind state. Some things you can tell yourself are:

"Others probably do care. They just may not be expressing it. Perhaps they do not know how to show their feelings. (Many people don't.) That doesn't mean they don't care."

Give Others the Benefit of the Doubt

You can make the decision to give others the benefit of the doubt. A friend of mine who had just graduated from college, an achievement he'd worked long and hard for, did not receive a single congratulations card or telephone call from his family or friends. Someone remarked, "Gee, you must feel really bad that no one cared enough to even send you a card." The sincere response of this success-minded friend was confidently matter-of-fact: "Not at all. I know they're thinking about me and proud of me."

Whether giving others the benefit of the doubt is justified is immaterial. Also understand that when others project inconsiderate or unkind thoughts and deeds, this behavior usually has more to do with them than you. Those who are in emotional pain or suffering often take it out on those around them. There are many reasons for a person's behaviors that are totally apart from his or her feelings about you. We know this, yet we are prone to forget it and fall into a self-pity party.

Pat Yourself on the Back

It's up to you to take charge of your state of mind. Pat yourself on the back for your efforts: for getting out of bed in the morning, for going to work, or for whatever you're doing as best you know how.

Recognize that what anyone else thinks about you matters little. What does matter are your beliefs about yourself and your choice of response. Demonstrating your concern for another's welfare is generally responded to in kind. However, if you find that those around you are on a track of ill will, keep in mind that it is their choice and their path. It need not be yours.

You always have a choice to accept or reject someone else's beliefs about you. Since nothing is served by accepting the negative judgments of others for yourself, don't. And this applies even if you agree they are right. Beliefs and facts, as we'll discuss shortly, are never cut in stone; they are merely the clay from which reality is formed, and you are the creator. You have the freedom to mold your personal reality in the best way you see fit, for your enhancement and well-being. So lift your head up and give yourself all the pats on the back and appreciation you need.

Faulty Belief Pattern No. 4
Half the time, what I do turns out all wrong. I always seem to fall short of perfection or fail.

Although few of us have done much reflection on the self-talk of thoughts and beliefs we feed ourselves when we "fail" (make a mistake, get an unwanted outcome), far too many of us see these transgressions as a reflection of who we are—bad, stupid, someone who can't do anything right—instead of simply what it is: a learning experience.

Instead of viewing an unwanted outcome as simply an event or feedback or a learning experience, people falling into this belief pattern have linked themselves to failure. When they take a risk and it doesn't turn out as they'd like, they see themselves as failures. Instead of congratulating themselves for taking the risk, irrespective of the outcome, they tie their identify to the event with a negative label and judgments of failure, wrong, ineptness and the like.

It's Okay to Make Mistakes

Perhaps no one has told them that the more successful they are destined to be, the more mistakes they're going to make. Highly successful, curious persons make more mistakes than anyone. You cannot learn to play the piano well without going through a lot of clanking and hitting wrong notes. You cannot become a pro tennis player without knocking a lot of balls out of bounds. You cannot become a success in your own business or career without experiencing many bumps and ups and downs. The secret is not in how many times you fall down, but how quickly you pick yourself up, learn from the event and continue toward your goals.

Redefine Feelings of Fear as Excitement

It's okay to feel anxious and be afraid or nervous in the face of risk, taking new actions or learning new skills and competencies. Even top actors and Olympic gold medal performers admit to anxiety before an important performance. It's not okay to allow that fear to immobilize you or prevent you from taking the action needed to reach your goals. When faced with feelings of fear or anxiety, relabel them in a more positive light as "excitement," or "massive energy."

Take Calculated Risks and Stop Worrying About the Outcome

Because of the strong, unpleasant emotions linked to our labels of defeat and failure, it isn't enough just to change the way we define the unwanted events in our life. We need the impetus of desire to take further action, even in the face of possible future failure. We are unlikely to take any risks if we believe that the probability of eventual success is unlikely or there is going to be little payoff. That is, if we believe that the price we have to pay is greater than the benefits we're going to receive, why take the risk?

The idea is not to take foolish risks where there is little to be gained. It is to let go of any fears and self-reprisals that are preventing you from acting in your best interests. Resolve to release those fears that are blocking your learning, growth and enjoyment of all life has to offer. Get prepared, make a reasonable cost-reward assessment and take the plunge. Stop worrying about falling short of perfection or failing.

Faulty Belief Pattern No. 5
Nothing I do seems to make much difference anyway. Why bother? I guess success is just not in the cards for me.

We need the belief that our actions and our efforts matter whether or not they lead to the hoped-for results. It is in the process of taking steps in the direction of your hopes and dreams that you grow and learn. Reaching a worthwhile goal may feel good temporarily, but it is the actions we take and efforts we make toward that goal that count the most in our favor.

The more you do with direction and in good faith, the greater the overall payoff. Many times what we do, and the incredible mistakes we make, are preparing us for a larger goal. Unwanted outcomes might also be telling us that we're on the wrong road and it's time to change directions. Get into the habit of welcoming the feedback you receive so that you can assess what adjustments need to be made.

When you get into thought patterns that plant seeds of doubt about the value of making the effort or taking steps toward your goals, you'll see this reflected in your emotional climate. Instead of an upbeat, high-energy enthusiasm for the challenges of life, you'll fall into a low ebb feeling of heaviness and struggle. Every task becomes a chore, tedious, irritating and bothersome.

This "don't care" pattern is one of the most devastating to taking constructive action and following through on our goals. If we believe our efforts do not matter and that what we do doesn't make much difference anyway, how are we possibly going to have the energy and enthusiasm to live a rich, full creative life?

Counteracting Self-Defeating Belief Patterns

The route to knocking out these self-defeating patterns lies in acquiring the powerful belief clusters and thinking habits of successful living. Rather than have you spend precious time figuring out the sources of unproductive thought patterns and ferreting them out, you will start building a storehouse of new success beliefs. Few of us have the time, skills, or even inclination to go through the painstaking process of digging into our past experiences. And there is no need. Your time is best spent on discovering and practicing what's right, rather than what's wrong.

As you learn to expand on more empowering patterns and discard the old unproductive ways, this will gradually become a natural habit. You will then find yourself progressing easily from desire states to taking the appropriate actions toward your goals. The ongoing battle with yourself and the struggle to get from point A to point B, to constantly have to jump start and kick yourself into gear, will dissolve into a stance of harmony and unity. The stressful gap between what you'd like to do and what you manage to get done will ease so that you flow smoothly from any current unwanted conditions to those more desirable conditions.

It is time to begin mastering the key principles of success and the mighty beliefs that power them.

Chapter 6
Key Ideas

1. The incompatibility of fulfilling your creative purpose while having financial well-being is an illusion sustained by your beliefs.

2. "Not enough time" is generally a bogus reason for not achieving our goals. Failure to take constructive action lies in a cluster of faulty beliefs centered around ourselves, such as what we believe about our competencies and feel we deserve.

3. Dwelling on the belief that "no one cares about you and what you do" leads nowhere and is best dropped. When you are grounded in solid beliefs about your own value as a person, pats on the back and approval from others are unnecessary. Focus on giving to others what you seek.

4. It makes no difference how many times you fail or make mistakes. The only real failure is to give up.

5. When you start believing that your efforts and actions do not matter, you are in serious trouble. Life matters. You matter. Take a small step each day in the direction of your goals.

"Don't stop trying; remember it is always the last key that opens the lock."
—Orison Swett Marden

III
SUCCESS PRINCIPLES & BELIEFS

"Some things have to be believed to be seen."
—Ralph Hodgson

Chapter 7

The Principle of Purpose

"The great and glorious masterpiece of man is to know how to live to purpose."
—Montaigne

Success Principles and Beliefs

Most of us are familiar with various principles of success. We've learned that in order to prosper and live a rewarding life we need to have a purpose, set goals, have the courage to take some risks and persevere until we achieve our objectives. What we haven't been told is how to implement these principles. Where does the courage to act in the face of our fears come from? Why are some people able to persevere until they complete their important goals in spite of tough obstacles, hardship and all kinds of problems? What is the life and energy behind these success barometers?

In the next few chapters we'll expand on five of these principles of success and examine the important personal beliefs that support them. Until these underlying beliefs become second nature to you, an integral part of your self-talk and thinking, little change is possible. Knowing what is required, that you need to have courage or vision or tenacity in order to be successful, only takes you so far. Acquiring the powerful beliefs upon which these principles stand is the key.

The first and most vital of the success principles is having a strong sense of purpose. Your purpose is then sustained and enacted by adopting the beliefs that underlie and power it.

Discovering Your Purpose

Your purpose is your mission in life, what you feel compelled to do, accomplish or be. Having a strong sense of purpose is what gives direction to your life.

Most of us take too many detours and scatter ourselves. We let a lot of little concerns grab our time, burn up our energy and throw us off course. By staying within the boundaries of our purpose we attend to those things that truly matter.

Your purpose in life is much broader and more general than your goals. For example, my purpose is to educate, inspire and empower as many people as possible. I do this through setting goals within that purpose, such as giving seminars, teaching classes, seeing clients and writing books.

Your purpose could evolve around a creative product or service—such as artwork, music or sports. It could relate to your family, an educational venture, health and fitness, or a business enterprise.

We discover our purpose via our curiosities and those things that are most important to us. It is your aim in life.

Robert Browning, the insightful poet, wrote, "The aim, if reached or not, makes great the life..." If you think about ships and airplanes, they never go in an arrow straight line toward their destination. They are continually correcting. You might say they are always off course. It is their aim, however, that gets them where they want to go.

A Reason to Live

Dr. Viktor Frankl, a German Jewish psychiatrist who wrote *Man's Search for Meaning* had a strong sense of purpose and it's what he attributes to keeping him alive and sane. He was one of the few survivors of the Nazi concentration camps and endured the horrors of watching tens of thousands go to their deaths. His story goes to the heart of how our thinking and beliefs can affect us.

In the concentration camp as a prisoner, he had virtually no freedom. He was subjected to inhuman treatment and torture. Typically, he received a tiny bowl of broth to eat daily.

Yet, what he came to realize was, that while he had no freedom to change his circumstances, the one ultimate freedom was his choice of thoughts to think and what to focus his mind upon. He knew that in spite of his conditions, he had the power to focus his mind on whatever he wanted.

So, he decided that instead of focusing on the despair of the situation, he would think about the good things he'd had in his life. Drawing on his memories, he focused his thoughts on his family—especially his wife, and her loving nature.

He gave himself a reason to live. He desperately wanted to see her again.

Rather than dwelling on the horrendous conditions of the concentration camp, he filled his mind with happy thoughts of the past, and hopeful thoughts for the future.

He took charge of his mind and consciously, intentionally shifted his thinking away from the unbearable conditions over which he had no control, to the pleasant memories of being with his family and friends.

Throughout the duration of his imprisonment, that was what he thought about and gave his attention to, with the little mental energy he had left.

And this is what he attributes to keeping him alive—to

once again be united with his family.

We Let Too Many Little Things Bog Us Down

Now, it's unlikely that you will ever have to endure such extreme circumstances, yet so many of us go through life letting minor incidents upset us, deplete our energy, and throw us off course.

Traffic jams, someone's critical words, poor service at a store or restaurant, can all too easily get us in a dither and ruin our day.

Even I am not always immune. One morning, I was walking down a sidewalk in Carmel, California, late for an important speaking engagement at The Pine Inn. I'd stopped to pick up a much-needed cup of coffee and had barely taken two sips when all of a sudden a bird fluttered over me and I heard this "plop."

I looked down and there it was, pu pu, right in my coffee. Yuck, a great way to start the day, I thought, and my initial reaction was definitely not amusement.

Later that day someone told me the story of a Midwest tourist couple who were walking along the sidewalk of the Ala Wai Blvd. in Honolulu one afternoon. Now this is a street lined with coconut trees. Suddenly without warning two coconuts dropped on their heads killing them both instantly. Now that's a tragedy! As farfetched as this sounds, it actually happened and made news across the nation. You may have heard about it. They have since trimmed the trees back along the Ala Wai and other places, so you needn't be worried about your next trip to Hawaii.

Your Purpose Keeps You on Target

When we have a strong sense of purpose in our lives, it helps us keep our perspective, so that we don't get bugged, bogged down and stressed out by all the little things.

Everyone has a purpose. It may not be a grand purpose like Mohandas Gandhi's or Mother Teresa's, but we all have a purpose to fulfill, whether it be small or large. That's why we're here.

If you're uncertain about your purpose, begin by looking to those things that you have a natural curiosity about, the things you are most interested in and value. If you haven't already, set some goals for yourself. Goals, recall, are more specific than your purpose. You need to set goals in all areas of your life—within the financial realm, in your career, with your family and relationships; fitness and health goals; even recreation and retirement goals. To begin, target the area of your life that you are currently most concerned about.

For many of us, this is the financial dimension. It is important to be specific about your goals. What does financial success mean to you? One million dollars? Two million? A five-bedroom home in Maui? A new red Corvette? A lear jet? More vacation time and leisure? Detail your financial dreams.

The critical question however is, "What gives some of us the impetus to act, move in the direction of our purpose, set goals and come out ahead, while others kick back, procrastinate and hope that somehow, someway, their ship will come in?

Powerful Beliefs to Keep You on Purpose

There are three simple but powerful beliefs that will help you stay on course and follow through on your goals.

A Solid Belief in Your Goals

Belief #1: First, is the belief that your purpose and goals are important.

If you don't have a solid belief in the goals you've laid out for yourself—that they are worthwhile in some way—you'll have little incentive to go after them.

Whatever your purpose or goals might be, you need to believe in them. You need to have a deep conviction that they are important.

Your Choices and Actions Count

Belief #2: The second belief to install in your mind is the belief that your decisions and actions make a difference, regardless of the outcome, that is, regardless of whether you make mistakes, fall on your face or everything goes wrong.

You want to instill the belief that every intentional action taken in good conscience matters. Every effort you make counts, irrespective of mistakes, errors, or mishaps.

Maybe you won't always get the job, the date, or the promotion. Maybe the speech you give will flop and the business you start go under.

Things don't always go smoothly. That's life.

Yet many of us act as if our life should continuously be one big dessert platter. And when it isn't, we throw a temper tantrum and cry, "Woe is me."

Get-Over-It and Get-On-with-It

But success is not about how many mistakes you make, or how many mishaps come your way, but how quickly you recover and continue on purpose toward your goals.

Every person that's ever accomplished anything worthwhile has made mistakes and failed at times. Many have had massive disasters strike, but that didn't deter them from their purpose and goals. When Thomas Edison was sixty-seven years old, his factory worth millions of dollars and containing a lifetime of work burned to the ground. Mr. Edison had nil insurance. His reaction? Sure he was upset, but he quickly recovered and said, "All our mistakes are burnt up. We will start building again tomorrow." Three weeks later he invented the phonograph.

Katherine Hepburn, winner of three Oscars, was rejected over and over again in her early screen interviews. She was told that her appearance was all wrong, that she had no talent whatsoever, and that she'd never make it as a movie star. But that didn't stop her from going on to becoming an award-winning actress.

Some of the greatest accomplishments in the world have been made by those who suffered tremendous hardships and difficulties.

John Milton wrote the classic, *Paradise Lost*, when he was living in abject poverty and was totally blind.

Julius Caesar, an epileptic, conquered the world.

Fyodor Dostoyevsky, the great philosopher and existentialist, lived in poverty, not knowing where his next meal was coming from.

Just Average?

But you say, these people are extraordinary. They're not like me. Me, I'm just average. Yet, practically every week in the news we hear about someone, just ordinary people, who have endured the worst possible conditions—a serious accident or illness, loss of a limb or loved one, bankruptcy and poverty—yet they go on to become an outstanding success in some field of endeavor. It's been said that "Setbacks are given to ordinary people to make them extraordinary."

All of these people started out just average like you and me. What made the difference was the absolute belief they had in themselves and what they were doing.

Give yourself the solid conviction that your efforts matter irrespective of what happens: irrespective of temporary setbacks, rejection, hardship or mistakes. There is nothing that can stop you if you believe. Walt Whitman, the American poet, wrote, "Nothing external has any power over me." He was in command of his thoughts, his beliefs and thereby, his life.

Move in the Direction of Your Goals

Belief #3: Finally, the third belief to implant is that all you ever need do is to take whatever action steps you currently know how in the direction of your purpose and goals.

Oliver Wendell Holmes reminds us, "The greatest thing in the world is not so much where we stand, as to what direction we are moving." You can correct as you go along. The important thing is to take aim and get started.

If you do not believe that your purpose and goals are important, or that the actions you take in their direction matter, you can be sure that the first time things go wrong or temptation knocks and distractions come along, you'll start wandering off course.

Plant Your Belief Seeds Deep

Plant these three belief seeds deep within your mind. Your purpose is important. It is what you are about. It is your life. If you haven't yet found your purpose, look for it. There is a reason you are here.

Your decisions and actions matter, regardless of the outcome. You can only do what you can do. And all you ever need do is take the steps that you know how at this point in time. You'll learn as you go along.

William James, the father of American psychology, and arguably one of the greatest psychologists and philosophers of all time tells us, "Our belief, at the beginning of an undertaking, is the *only thing* that insures the successful outcome of our venture."

By planting a solid inventory of beliefs in your mind, you'll be empowered to stay on course, and feel good about yourself no matter what curves life throws you.

Chapter 7
Key Ideas

1. There are a number of principles important to successful living; however, to implement them in your life you need to implant the beliefs that power them.

2. A vital principle of success is having a strong sense of purpose and setting goals within that purpose. Your purpose is activated by adopting the beliefs that underlie and sustain it.

3. Three powerful beliefs that will help you stay on purpose are: One, the belief that your purpose and goals are important; two, the belief that your decisions and actions matter regardless of the outcome; and three, the belief that all you ever need do is to take whatever action steps you currently know how in the direction of your purpose and goals.

4. Plant these beliefs in your mind today and begin reaping the rewards!

"Our life is what our beliefs make it."
—Author

Chapter 8

The Principle of Vision

"If you want to do great things you need to have a great vision."
—Author Unknown

Mental Imaging
A second key principle of success is vision, using our imagination for mental imaging.

The concept of vision is threefold: having a clear picture of your goals; seeing yourself moving toward your goals and objectives; and visualizing the benefits and rewards of achieving your desires and dreams.

Picture Your Goals
First is having a clear image of the specific goals embodied within your purpose. Let's say you have a concern for the health and welfare of people, and you have targeted your purpose as educating others in nutrition, diet and exercise. You might picture yourself involved in such goals as standing before a class of high school students talking about the hazards of smoking, or eating too much junk food.

Or you might see yourself meeting with prospective

clients and helping them to realize the benefits of the health products you are promoting. In other words, you have a mental image of your particular goal.

See Yourself Moving toward Your Goals

A second element of vision is maintaining a clear picture of yourself moving toward the goals within your purpose. In this example, you might see yourself at the library collecting data about nutrition and physical fitness. In your mind's eye you see yourself doing those things that lead to your goals and objectives, the end product. Success is most of all a journey. You want to see yourself "in the act" of progressing toward your goals.

Visualize the Benefits and Rewards

Finally, visualize the benefits and rewards you will have upon achieving your goals. Here you could see yourself going to the mailbox and receiving dozens of letters from students telling you how much you've helped them to stop smoking or to improve their diet. In your mind's eye, you see yourself reading the letters, feeling the joy and satisfaction of helping someone.

If the outcome of your goal is having more money, visualize all the ways in which your life will change for the better: a beautiful home and luxury car; more free time to spend with your family; money to travel and visit your out-of-town loved ones. Mentally picture and experience the joys of riches.

The goals you set will change during your lifetime. The idea is to have a sharp image of the particular goal facing you now.

Whether your goal is great or small, maintaining a vision is mandatory. When the first man was put on the moon, the question was asked, "How did you ever manage to accomplish such a feat?" The reply was, "With a thousand errors and knowing where we wanted to go. We kept our vision before us."

Beliefs to Sustain Your Vision

But keeping your vision before you, and not losing heart when things go wrong, all depends on the beliefs you harbor about yourself.

There are three important beliefs to give yourself to sustain your vision.

You Can Do It!

Belief #1: One, is a belief in your capabilities to make your goal a reality, that is, you believe you *can* do it. You believe that you have the necessary skills and competencies to follow through to completion. Or if you don't presently have the needed skills, you believe in your ability to acquire them. For instance, you can learn how to use the computer, improve your marketing skills, or hone your speaking skills.

You Will Do It!

Belief #2: Secondly, keeping a vision before you means you believe that you *will* do it. Belief in your potential to accomplish a goal is one thing. But your belief must also include the *willingness* to do whatever it takes to make your goal a reality (that is legal and moral of course).

Most of us believe that we have the potential to realize our goals. The majority of us believe that we *could* start a business, write a book, or make more money. And most of us tend to believe that we could eliminate those bad habits that are interfering with our goals, such as eating, smoking or drinking too much. But how many of us have a solid conviction that says, "It is not only possible; I am not only capable, but I am willing to go that extra mile to do it"?

You Deserve Success

Belief #3: Finally, to consistently keep a vision before you requires the supporting belief that you *deserve* this goal, that you are worthy of both the goal and any benefits or rewards which will follow as a result of its completion. If at a subconscious level you do not believe you deserve fame and fortune or whatever the rewards might be, your vision will fade long before it takes form.

Conrad Hilton was once asked when it was that he realized that he was truly wealthy. He replied, "I realized it when I was sleeping on park benches." Years before the Hilton hotel chain became a physical reality, it was a reality in the mind of Conrad Hilton, its creator. He had a vision. And more importantly, he believed in himself to make that vision happen.

Everything First Started in Someone's Imagination

Every physical object we see in our environment—whether it be hotels, airplanes, roller coasters, computers, or cars—first started in someone's mind, in their imagination. They had a vision, an image of it.

We take so many things for granted. We sometimes forget what life would be like without our inventions. In a recent survey, folks were asked to pick an invention that they could not live without. Interestingly, twice as many picked aspirin over a personal computer.

Can you imagine living without aspirins or Tylenol? Or music? Your television set? Toilet tissue? A bed to sleep in? Your car? Books to read? A toothbrush? A brush or comb? Deodorant?

Every physical object was first created in someone's imagination. They had a vision of it.

But lying deep beneath that vision and sustaining it to its completion was the mighty belief in their power to make that vision a reality.

Believe in Your Ideas and Yourself

I'd venture to say that at one time or another, you have had an idea in your imagination to do something or create something that hasn't been done yet. Yet how many of us believe in ourselves and our ideas enough to follow through on them?

Keeping your vision is predicated on a strong belief in yourself to make it happen. You believe in yourself totally, without reservation. You hold the belief that you will do it, no matter what.

You are unstoppable. You will do whatever it takes. Obstacles will be turned into opportunities; hardships make you more determined; mistakes teach you lessons and make you stronger. You, my reader, are the master of your destiny. Believe it and you will be proven right.

Finally, deep within your heart you believe you are deserving. You deserve all the rewards of your vision's fulfillment. Life was meant to be enjoyed and relished. It is your birthright to have a prosperous, happy, rewarding life. And so it is.

Chapter 8
Key Ideas

1. In order to achieve our goals, we need to keep our vision. Use your imagination to visualize your current goal. See yourself actually moving toward your desire. Picture the outcome of your efforts—the rewards and benefits.

2. To keep your vision and not lose heart when things go wrong depends on the beliefs you harbor about yourself.

3. Three potent beliefs to sustain your vision are: (1)a belief in your capabilities to make your goal a reality; (2)a willingness to do whatever it takes to make it happen; and (3)the belief that you deserve all the benefits and rewards of your goal's fulfillment.

4. You are the master of your destiny. Believe it and you will be proven right.

"There are so many wonderful things in your everyday experience, lucrative opportunities, glorious occasions, that do not exist for you because you do not have the vision for discerning them."
—Edward Kramer

Chapter 9

The Principle of Courage

"The greatest test of courage on the earth is to bear defeat
without losing heart."
—R. G. Ingersoll

The Faces of Courage

Courage can mean many different things. Courage doesn't
mean having no fears, but making the choice to act even in
the face of your fears. Courage means facing your fears and
refusing to let them interfere with your important goals.
Courage can mean taking a stand, or choosing to do what you
deem right even in the face of other people's disapproval,
opposing pressures or unpleasant consequences to yourself.

Courage is taking whatever small steps you can each day
toward your goals whether anyone else knows about it or pats
you on the back.

Courage can also mean living with a past mistake and not
letting guilt or remorse weigh you down and keep you from
your goals.

Perhaps one of the most important aspects of courage is
refusing to give up and persisting in the face of difficulties
and when everything goes wrong. This dimension of courage

is linked to the principle of perseverance, which we'll look at next.

Thus courage has many faces.

The Cornerstone of Courage

But what kinds of beliefs give you the courage to face your fears and act even when you're afraid?

What beliefs keep you going when you have no assurance of a positive outcome? When everything imaginable starts going wrong?

What gives you the courage and confidence to get started and go forward when you have no past history of success?

And how about when others don't believe in you? Not only don't believe in you but almost seem to delight in tearing you down, and telling you how utterly absurd your aspirations are?

At the cornerstone of courage are the beliefs you hold about success, failure and making mistakes. Many of us adhere to the motto, "If at first you don't succeed, give up. It's not worth it." Or, "When the going gets tough, take a vacation, or take a drink."

Courage Springs from a Host of Beliefs

Courageous acts, whether they are small or large, generally have a host of beliefs behind them, and the more, the better. We'll look at eight of these, beliefs found among those who have learned to contain their fears and consistently act with courage.

Act in the Face of Fear

Belief #1: "Though I am not fearless or may never be totally free of all fear, I believe that it is important to act even

116

in the face of my fears if it will move me closer to my goals. I know that fear vanishes when I take action and stare it in the face, instead of running away from it."

Mark Twain once said, "Courage is...mastery of fear—not absence of fear." Don't try to suppress your fears; make up your mind to act in the face of them.

Use Mind Power

Belief #2: "I also believe in my power of mind. I can and will take charge of my thoughts and actions to knock out any fears that arise. Nothing will prevent me from taking the appropriate steps toward my goals."

Notice how your mental strength magnifies, and how good you feel when you take in these beliefs!

Mistakes Are a Part of Learning

Belief #3: "I believe that mistakes and problems are a necessary part of life and learning. If I mess up and fall on my face, it's okay. I'll pat myself on the back for taking the risk."

Life and living are about problems, or more accurately, about challenges and opportunities. We need to remind ourselves when problems are bearing down on us, and no relief is in sight, that every problem arrives with a gift in its hand. For every door that closes, two more open. Helen Keller once observed, "Too often we're so focused on the door that closed, we're unable to see new ones opening."

Don't Let Others Deter You from Your Dreams

Belief #4: A fourth essential belief for courage has to do with those people in your life that are nonsupportive and negative.

When those you associate with are critical and unable to support you in your purpose and goals, give yourself this conviction: "I believe that if others have a problem with my mistakes and hopes and dreams...such as my spouse, friends, employer or children...that's *their* problem. It will in no way intimidate me, embarrass me or stop me from taking the necessary actions toward my goals."

Along with this, tell yourself, "I do not need the approval of others. Nor is my self-esteem, how I feel about myself, dependent on what others think and believe about me. I need always to only do my best and believe in myself."

Unconditional Self-Worth

Belief #5: At the foundation of courage is the belief that you are a worthy person under all conditions and circumstances. No matter what your current financial situation, what family or relationship problems you have, or how many mistakes and failures you've had, you are a worthy person.

Stop Judging Yourself

Stop judging yourself based on where you presently stand or past mistakes. Each of us is doing the best we know how. Be proud of whoever you are.

A friend of mind, a kind, loving, gracious lady in her fifties recently invited me out to meet her daughter, a psychology professor and graduate of Stanford University.

This lady, though in her fifties, looks terrific, is very active, and lives life to its fullest. She is always positive, never complaining about anything or anyone. I have a great deal of respect for her.

She's very proud of her children and grandkids, all of whom are well-educated and high achievers—one's a doctor, another an attorney and so on. Margie, on the other hand, has little formal education and has always been a homemaker.

When I arrived at the restaurant to meet her daughter, the Stanford graduate, I commented to the young girl, "You must be very proud of your mother. She's a terrific person."

My friend was visibly taken back, and looked at me in astonishment, "Proud of me? Oh, no," she said, "I'm proud of her."

The next day she called and said how touched she was by my comment, how she'd always felt insecure and inferior about being the only one in her family who didn't have a higher education and, in her words, hadn't "done anything with her life."

She never imagined that anyone could be proud of her. She wasn't proud of herself.

Accept Yourself Regardless of Circumstances

I had to remind her that having a higher education or an important job doesn't necessarily make you a better person. It's who you are inside that matters. Your value as a person, in any case, should never be contingent on a job or education or any other condition.

If you base your self-worth or esteem on conditions outside of yourself, you're always going to be on shaky ground because, as pointed out earlier, rarely will everything in your life be going perfectly. You get your finances in order, and your relationship takes a tumble, or vice versa. You find the perfect sweetheart, and you lose your job. Or everything is going along fine, and then your body starts falling apart.

You need to get clear with yourself that you are a worthy, deserving person in spite of any of the situations that befall you. We don't always have control over what happens to us, but we always, repeat, *always*, have control over how we define those events in relation to ourselves.

Act and Correct

Belief #6: A sixth conviction sustaining courage is: "I believe that our intentional acts count, irrespective of the outcome. I therefore use my best judgment and act even in the face of uncertainties. This does not mean I act foolhardily. I simply know that if I waited until all the information was in, or conditions were just right, I'd never get anything done. I therefore act and correct as I go along."

There will always be uncertainties. Life is never one hundred per cent foolproof. Prepare yourself as best you know how; make an intelligent assessment of the situation and plunge in. Your efforts *will* be rewarded—if not on the first try, then the next or the next. Believe it is so. Learn from your mistakes and keep at it.

Fear of Success?

Belief #7: Some of us don't fear failure so much, but we have a greater fear of success, and all the responsibilities and challenges that go along with it. Each time we find ourselves right on the verge of achieving a major success, we do something to sabotage it. This is one I personally can attest to. On a number of occasions I've been right on the verge of achieving a major success and pulled back, afraid I wouldn't be able to handle the responsibilities of massive success.

Many years ago when my first book was published, I was plagued with thoughts like, "What if it becomes a best seller? I'll have to go on all the major television talk shows and will be influencing millions of people. It's a wonderful opportunity to help others, but what if I get nervous and say something stupid and harm someone? And what will my children think of me if I flub up? Working with individual clients is great, but being a best-selling celebrity is scary." I was filled with self-doubts about my capabilities to handle all the challenges and responsibilities that arise from success.

How did I get over it? Saw a psychologist of course! Actually, I came to the realization that we're never given more challenges or responsibilities than we can handle. No, we may not always deal with the newfound success perfectly. And mistakes will be made. But that's no excuse for throwing in the towel. I knew that I had knowledge which could help thousands of people live a happier and more rewarding life. All I needed to overcome my fear of success was exactly as for you: a solid belief in my ability to handle any situation that arose.

Firmly implant a conviction that you are capable of handling whatever challenges might arise from your newfound success. Give yourself the belief: "I will not only be able to handle any failures that come my way, I will also be able to handle the new responsibilities that come with greater success."

Mistakes Are Part of Learning

Belief #8: Finally, the eighth belief cluster to nurture in your mind relates to dealing with your mistakes and mishaps.

Tell yourself, "I believe that the more I do, the faster I'll learn. The more actions I take in the direction of my goals, the more I'm going to accelerate their realization. Likewise, the more I do, the more mistakes I'm likely to make. This is part of the territory of learning, growing and achieving outstanding success."

Double Your Failure Rate

It has been said, "If you want to succeed, double your failure rate." If you're out there doing things, you're going to make mistakes. Remind yourself that "It's not how often you fall into the puddle that matters, but how quickly you're able to climb out."

Everyone that's ever been highly successful has experienced failure, loads of failures.

In basketball, professional players only make about half of their shots. We could say that they failed half of the time. In football, the best quarterbacks complete only six out of ten passes.

Some of the most successful actors and actresses get turned down in over eighty per cent of their auditions. In other words, they are failing eighty per cent of the time. Many sales men and women report that they get rejected nine times out of ten.

Babe Ruth, the great American batter, struck out more than any other player, 1,330 times. But we don't remember him for his strikeouts. We remember him for his record number of home runs.

Redefine Your Failures

It's not if you fail or how often you fail, but your perception and interpretation of that failure. Thomas Edison, when asked how he could continue in view of his hundreds of failures, replied, "I have not failed once." He regarded his so-called failures as "feedback," "a learning experience." He was learning what didn't work. The criticism and ridicule of others didn't faze him. He believed in himself and his efforts.

Alfred Adler, the gifted philosopher, once said, "We are not so much influenced by 'facts' but by our interpretations of facts, that is, by our perceptions and beliefs about them." The solution to any problem lies in choosing to see it differently.

How we choose to view our mistakes and the mishaps of life makes all the difference, both in how we feel and how we respond to the situation.

The more of these eight beliefs that you can add to your mind's reservoir, the easier it will be to act with courage; and the more you'll accelerate your personal growth and the achievement of your goals.

Beliefs Can Bring Disaster or Success

Your mind is constantly manufacturing thoughts, opinions and beliefs. Emerson once remarked, "We are born believing. Our brain manufactures beliefs like a tree grows apples." We have witnessed in our society how pervasive a person's beliefs can be. Beliefs can prompt someone to commit cowardly hate crimes, senseless acts of violence and even murder. Our beliefs can put us into a state of despair, defeat and depression. But we also know that our personal beliefs can lead us to success, joyful living, better relationships, financial independence and other positive outcomes.

Only you can decide which ones you will allow to hang around in your mind. Only you can decide which beliefs to give your attention to and dwell upon. Only you can select, eject and direct your mind's thoughts and beliefs and change your life. You are the director and controller of your mind's assets and liabilities. And according to these, lies your fate and fortune.

Chapter 9
Key Ideas

1. At the cornerstone of courage are the beliefs you hold about success and failure.

2. A host of personal success beliefs are found among those who have learned how to contain their fears and consistently act with courage.

3. Your mind is constantly producing thoughts and beliefs. Some of these lead to despair and defeat. Others lead to courageous acts, happiness and success. It is up to you to decide which ones you will allow to hang around in your mind.

"All our dreams can come true if we have the courage to pursue them."
—Walt Disney

Chapter 10

The Principle of Perseverance

*"There is nothing which persevering effort and unceasing
and diligent care cannot overcome."*
—Lucius Annaeus Seneca

Winners Persevere
The principle of perseverance has often been said to be one
of the most critical to achieving great success.

Perseverance is continuing toward your goals "in spite of,"
in spite of all the problems that crop up, or the distractions
and temptations that get in the way. It is refusing to give up
whether you're feeling tired or sick, when doubts creep in, or
when everything goes awry.

When Murphy's law strikes with everything going wrong
at the least opportune time, the winner becomes even more
determined. Perseverance has been likened to the postage
stamp; it sticks to something until it arrives at its final destination.

Persisting toward your hopes and dreams in the face of obstacles, temptations and distractions is only possible if you
have established a solid foundation of beliefs about yourself
and life's events. You need to have a battery of beliefs, deep
personal convictions that will keep you going no matter what.

While the personal beliefs underlying perseverance depend to some extent on your goals, your personal values and what motivates you, there are a number of powerful beliefs that perseverance is built upon.

Beliefs to Keep You Going No Matter What

Here are eight beliefs to keep you persisting toward your dreams no matter how many rejections, obstacles and hurdles come your way. Begin making them a part of your thinking now.

Your Life Will Change for the Better

Belief #1: The first is that your life will change for the better. You believe that, in one way or another, persevering toward your goals will have a positive outcome. Your focus is on the outcome, the prize, not the hardships or price you may have to pay. Your life *is* going to change for the better. Believe it and it will happen.

Your Activities Make a Difference

Belief #2: A second belief to install is "What I'm doing makes a difference." Perhaps it will help people in some way. If you're promoting health products, it can improve their physical as well as mental well-being. If you are in the insurance business, you are giving people security and peace of mind. If you are an educator, you are helping to reduce ignorance and prejudice. If you are in real estate, you're putting a roof over someone's head, and giving them the pride of home ownership. Whatever your activities, firmly believe that what you're doing makes a difference.

You Are Accomplishing Your Goals

Belief #3: The third strong conviction to give yourself is "I am accomplishing the goals I've targeted." You believe, purely and simply, that this is a fact, a given. For most everyone, the culmination of reaching a goal that they have set is rewarding and a victory in itself, regardless of what it is or how small it might be.

You are accomplishing the goals you've targeted *now.* Mentally accept it. Feel it. Live it.

Enjoy the Journey

Belief #4: Tell yourself, "I will reap many rewards from my journey toward this goal. My persistence will pay off in joy, happiness, feeling better, or some other desirable state. It will pay off both as a I make progress and upon completion." You feel a sense of satisfaction in regularly progressing toward your goal. Acknowledging this, even when the completion date is a long way off, keeps you on track. You know how you'd feel if you gave up, or let yourself continually get sidetracked. You believe in the process, the rich satisfaction of having control over your direction in life.

You Finish What You Start

Belief #5: "It is important to finish what I start."

Those who hold this belief are generally successful in completing what they start. They can't hold themselves back when this belief is planted deeply in their minds. Like a magnet, they are irresistibly drawn toward their goal and its completion. You too are finishing what you start. It is important, and you know it.

We Act as We Are

Belief #6: Along with this is the belief: "I am not a quitter; I'm a winner." This belief is tied to your self-concept. Winners don't quit. When you have a firm conviction about yourself that you are not someone who gives up until the job is done, it's much easier to move toward your goals. We act as we are. Your behaviors are a natural extension of the beliefs that you harbor about yourself.

Henry David Thoreau once said, "Live your beliefs and you can turn the world around." Certainly, you can turn your life around.

Your Efforts Matter

Belief #7: It is worthwhile to persist even if the chances of success sometimes seem remote or far away in the distant future.

You believe that your efforts matter even when you're unable to reach your goals. You've probably heard the saying by Robert Browning, "Ah, but a man's reach should exceed his grasp, or what's a heaven for?" You are convinced that every step you take in the direction of your goals counts, regardless of the outcome.

Having this belief to fall back on is highly useful for goals that are a long way off, or when Doubting Thomas jumps up on your shoulder and you seem to be making little or no progress. Zig Zigler, the popular motivational speaker, once said, "When we give it our all we can live with ourselves, regardless of the outcome."

Fill Your Time with Worthwhile Goals

Belief #8: Finally, an eighth useful belief comes to us from CNN entrepreneur Ted Turner. When asked about his work, he said, "I need to fill my time and life with something. It may as well be challenging goals."

We all have a choice about what we fill our lives with, whether it be trivial pursuits and unproductive activities, or worthwhile goals. And your beliefs determine exactly what that life will be.

The more beliefs, such as these eight that you implant and keep dominant in your mind, the easier it will be to persist, regardless of life's setbacks and uncertainties.

To solidify the importance and impact that these beliefs can have on your life, take a moment to consider their opposites.

What if you continually focused on beliefs and thoughts such as: "Nothing I do makes any difference. I can never seem to finish what I start. I guess I'm a loser. All that work and it's probably not going to matter anyway." How far do you think you'd go with this kind of mental makeup?

Giving yourself a supportive set of beliefs to call upon when you need them acts as a powerful driving force for the completion of your tasks, and the realization of your goals and objectives.

Too Often We Stop Just Short of Success

Far too many of us stop trying and give up just short of arriving at an important goal and success. Often just a little more effort, a little more perseverance, will make the difference between being a runner-up and a champion.

Dr. Venice Bloodworth in her best-selling book, *Key to Yourself*, tells the parable of the little boy that went off on a journey to find the Wishing Gate.

He was so wrapped up in finding it that he didn't notice where he was going and soon discovered that he was lost. He became tired and sat down on an old stile to rest.

The North Wind came along and offered to take him home. Since he was tired and hungry and discouraged, he took the North Wind up on his offer, abandoning his quest.

As they were traveling along, the North Wind asked him how he came to be lost. The boy replied that he was looking for the Wishing Gate.

The North Wind laughed all the rest of the way home.

When they arrived at the boy's home, the North Wind said to him, "The next time you go out searching for something, keep your wits about you. You were sitting on the Wishing Gate when I found you."

How often have you been right there, practically on top of something, on the verge of realizing an important goal, but you missed out on it for one reason or another? Maybe it was a super new job, a good relationship, or an investment opportunity that would have made your life a whole lot easier.

The Smart Rat

In psychological research, there's a phenomenon called "the smart rat."

The first day that rats are put in a maze to find cheese, the smart rat is able to find the hidden cheese very quickly...lickety split...he's off and running, zipping through the maze along the shortest possible route, and in the shortest time.

On the second day, the smart rat will go directly to the place where the cheese was the day before. When he sees no cheese there (the devious psychologist has taken it away), the rat stops and looks around puzzled, as if to say, "Where's the cheese? It's supposed to be here. What's wrong with this maze today anyway?"

The rat then sits down and waits for the cheese to be delivered—and in fact, he will sit there...waiting for the cheese to arrive...until he starves to death.

130

Meanwhile, in the next tunnel over stands the cheese. A few more moves and he would have had it and been an alive, happy and fulfilled rat.

Like the "smart" rat, often we stay stuck in old patterns, things that worked in the past but are no longer working. Instead of venturing out on different paths, we wait in vain for something to change. We wait for our ship to come in. Our limiting beliefs tell us, "It worked before. Why not now?" We put ourselves at the mercy of the conditions of our environment instead of opening our minds to new possibilities and persisting.

Beliefs Are a Powerful Driving Force

A story is told about Chinese farmers who planted bamboo on their farms. The first year, they all watered and weeded the ground, but nothing came up. Many of the farmers gave up.

The second year the remaining farmers continued to water and weed the ground, still nothing came up. More of the farmers quit, dug up the ground and planted other crops.

The third year, a few of the farmers continued to nurture their bamboo ground. But again, no bamboo appeared.

By the fourth year only three farmers had persevered, continuing to believe in their crop and tend to the soil. Another year passed, and nothing. No bamboo broke ground.

Finally, one lone farmer remained in that fifth year, and you know what happened? A million miles of root systems had spread underneath the ground. And when the bamboo broke through the earth that fifth year, it grew more than a foot a day.

In just six weeks, it was more than sixty feet tall!

The farmer who continued to believe that his efforts would pay off and persisted harvested the bamboo and became extremely wealthy.

Believe That Your Efforts Will Pay Off

That extra effort which some of us have to persist when things go wrong or there is no visible sign of progress, makes the difference between the loser and the winner, the runner up and the champion.

And that extra effort lies in your thoughts and beliefs, mind tools that you have control over, and the power to change and charge up in accord with your fondest dreams.

Even minute changes in your beliefs will often result in momentous changes in your life. Nothing can stop the person whose mind is stocked with solid beliefs. Dreams come true when built on a solid foundation of beliefs.

Choose to believe in yourself and what you're doing. Know that your life can and will change for the better. You are someone who finishes what you start. You are not a quitter. You're a winner. It's your time and your life, and you have the power to call it as you choose.

Decide today to choose those beliefs about yourself and life that will advance you toward your desires and dreams.

Chapter 10
Key Ideas

1. Of all the principles of success, perseverance is the most important to achieving outstanding success.

2. Perseverance is built upon a solid foundation of success beliefs. Making these beliefs a part of your thinking and living will keep you moving toward your dreams no matter how many rejections, failures, or obstacles come your way.

3. You have the power *right now* to begin building a new set of beliefs and rapidly advancing toward your desires and dreams.

"The champion does his best, then he does a little more."
—Author Unknown

Chapter 11

The Principle of Passion

*"A person can succeed at almost anything for which he
has unlimited enthusiasm."*
—**Charles Schaub**

Fired Up!
The final success principle we'll look at is passion.

Passion has to do with your enthusiasm and energy. It is
your emotional involvement, having such a high level of interest in what you're doing that you find yourself almost
magically drawn to the goal. You simply cannot resist taking
action. Passion is closely tied to your purpose in life.

Passion is a desire so strong it has been likened to the
heating process that takes place inside a black walnut.

When the life inside the hard shell of the black walnut
starts to heat up, nothing can hold it back. It breaks open the
hard, stone-like shell of the walnut as if it were flimsy paper,
sending out a shoot through earth that grows into a giant walnut tree.

When we get fired up inside and have a powerful passion
to accomplish something, nothing can hold us back. We can
accomplish the seemingly impossible.

A story is told about a young man who came to see

Socrates and asked him the secret to success. Socrates told the boy to meet him near the river the next day. They met and Socrates asked the young man to walk with him into the river.

When the water got up to their necks, Socrates took the young man by surprise and dunked him into the water. The boy struggled to get out, but Socrates was strong and kept him under until the boy started turning blue. Then Socrates quickly pulled his head out of the water. The first thing the young man did was to gasp and take a deep breath of air.

Socrates asked him, "What did you want the most when you were underwater?" The boy replied, "Air."

Socrates then said, "That is the secret to success. When you want success as badly as you wanted the air, then you'll get it."

How Much Do You Want Success?

How badly do you want success? How much do you want a million dollars? A dream home? A new car? A better relationship?

Having a burning desire is essential to creating massive success. Just like a small fire doesn't give off much heat, a weak desire doesn't produce great results.

When you want something badly enough, whether it's a new exciting career, attracting the right person and having a better relationship, or even millions of dollars, you're almost certain to get it.

Bored and Distracted

The pivotal question is: Where does this burning desire, this passion come from? Many of us are almost apathetic about our goals and our daily life. Clients will frequently tell me how bored they are with everything—their work, their friends, their mate—their life.

To escape from this boredom, we get caught up in all the distractions of modern day living, going to happy hour every night, drinking too much, smoking or eating too much, and watching one violent show after another on television or at the movies. Life becomes a series of unfulfilling and unproductive events that fill up the hours.

What is the critical difference between those high-energy, success-bound individuals and those who drift through life bored and unfulfilled? Why are so few people powered by passion, energy and enthusiasm while the majority of the population lays back, taking whatever life dishes out, largely making decisions by default?

Personal Beliefs That Power Passion

A belief sequence I've observed over and over again among those who consistently move passionately and excitedly toward their goals is simply this: *"I believe what I'm doing is important. My goals make a difference. I make a difference. My choices and efforts and actions truly matter."*

You are unlikely to have unbridled passion toward your goals if you don't believe that they are important or worthwhile. You are unlikely to stay excited and enthused unless you are convinced that what you're doing matters, or that you will receive some benefit from your actions.

We can only pump ourselves up with enthusiasm and courage and perseverance from external sources for so long. Unless we have established the deep inner personal beliefs that give life to these principles, they'll be short-lived and ineffective.

Potent Belief Threads

What you've probably noticed by now is a common thread of beliefs that run through all the principles of successful living. Some of these beliefs are more potent than others, yielding a reverberating effect over many facets of our life.

"Having a strong sense of mission, knowing that you are here for a reason, and that the choices you make and actions you take genuinely matter irrespective of the outcome" is one of the most powerful belief combinations you can hold.

Another is a deep conviction that you are a worthy, deserving person and that your life has value and meaning.

Empowering Beliefs Will Change Your Life

Our mind's resources, our thoughts, images and beliefs are invisible like the wind and electricity, yet their power can be even greater. Until we learned how to harness the powers of wind and electricity, they were of little use to us. We were largely at the mercy of their adverse effects.

Until we learn how to make better use of those invisible aspects of ourselves, the thoughts and beliefs that inhabit our minds, we will mostly be slaves to their negative effects.

Every truly successful person has learned how to tap into this mighty realm of the unseen, and to mold his or her thoughts and beliefs in accord with the outcomes desired. Your beliefs and thoughts are the cause agents; the conditions of your life are the effect.

It is your choice and your human right and privilege to select and settle into your mind a success network of personal beliefs. There is no need to continue to let self-sabotaging beliefs based upon insecurity, doubt and fear dictate your destiny, jeopardizing your happiness and well-being.

Our greatest human gift is our conscious power of choice—the choice to decide on the content of our mind; the choice to decide what we will focus on and what we will dismiss; the choice to stop letting self-defeating beliefs run our lives; the choice to embrace those beliefs that carry us easily and effortlessly toward our hopes and dreams.

Empowering beliefs can become as natural and automatic to your thinking and living as breathing. And when they do, success is virtually guaranteed. Make the choice now to let go of polluted and contaminated beliefs and change your life.

Chapter 11
Key Ideas

1. Passion has to do with your enthusiasm and energy. It is closely related to the your purpose in life.

2. Those who move consistently and passionately toward their dreams believe that what they're doing is important. They believe that their goals make a difference, and that they make a difference. They are convinced that their choices and efforts and actions truly matter.

3. A common thread of beliefs runs through all the principles of successful living.

4. Building the powerful personal belief clusters that support these success principles will make your dreams a reality.

"Believing in yourself and what you're doing is the most important rung on the ladder of success."
—Author

Chapter 12

Potent Belief Clusters

***"Believe that life is worth living, and your belief will help
create the fact."***
—William James

Core Belief Clusters for Happiness and Successful Living
You are now well on the way to building a solid foundation
of empowering beliefs. You are beginning to think and act
like a winner. A better life is in the making. It is time to pull
together some of the ideas we've been discussing and look at
a number of core belief patterns that lie at the heart of true
happiness and successful living.

In this chapter, we'll look specifically at four potent belief
families: (1)the beliefs you hold about the world in which
you live; (2)beliefs about the events of your life—those
things that happen to you and how you interpret them;
(3)beliefs about others; and most importantly, (4)those beliefs you hold about yourself.

Some of the beliefs listed may be difficult for you to adopt
into your mind's current storehouse of facts. While every
belief can be questioned, disputed or rejected, try to view the
ideas in terms of their value for your life, i.e., their consequences. For example, a personal belief in an irrational,

unpredictable, hostile world has one consequence for your life. Belief in a rational, purposive and benevolent world has a totally different effect on your life. If you believe people are basically untrustworthy, this will be reflected in the quality of your interpersonal relationships. If you believe you are undeserving of kindness and love, this will have a marked effect on what you receive. If you believe you have little control over your life, the consequences will be entirely different than if you believe you are the director of your fate.

Dealing with Doubts

In some instances, you might logically protest, "How can I possibly accept this belief? It doesn't ring true based on what I know." The response to make to yourself is this: "Okay, based on what I know now, it doesn't sound plausible. On the other hand, I know that everyone's slice of reality, set of truths about the world and themselves, differs depending on his culture, family background, education and past experiences, so who am I to judge that my particular set of facts is right and another is wrong? Actually, I don't need to judge at all. I can decide to adopt a belief strictly on the merit of its benefits, that is, the kind of results I'm likely to get from this belief over another one."

You might also deal with your current logical mind of facts by instructing yourself to set it aside temporarily and allow for the possibility of a new way of thinking. You always have the power to step outside the realm of your preexisting mindset and "try on" another kind of mind attire. If you find it works, keep it; if not, you can always shed it. In the next chapter, you'll be given a dynamic mind strategy to assist you in the change process.

It is not my place to tell you what to believe. However, I hope to influence you to keep a portion of your mind open to those beliefs that enrich you rather than hinder or disable you. Remember, minds are like parachutes—they only function when open.

Your Worldview

What kind of a world do you see yourself living in? Is it friendly? Unfriendly? Intelligent and benevolent, or random and unpredictable? Is there any meaning to life on this earth? Is there a purpose to our world? Many of our beliefs in this area are only roughly defined; nonetheless, we all have impressions that affect us. Some of the belief impressions we hold leave us feeling uneasy and fearful. Others provide us with a sense of wonder and expansion.

The beliefs you harbor here can have dramatic and far-reaching consequences for your life. More than one prominent person in history has been driven to the brink of insanity by a line of reasoning and beliefs in a fundamentally meaningless, hostile and unpredictable world. Other thinkers have been inspired to greatness by their interpretations of the universe.

The beliefs identified below have the power to change your life if they are accepted. Methods to allow for the possibility of their acceptance into your mind are given in the next chapter. At this reading, you need only consider their beneficial value.

Potent Belief Cluster One

1. There is purpose and meaning in life.
2. The world is basically friendly, benevolent and evolving harmoniously.
3. We live in a universe of abundance.

When Albert Einstein was asked what he believed the most important question to ask was, he responded, "Is the universe friendly?" We are a part of an alive, purposeful, evolving universe. Both our mental and physical health are affected by the beliefs we hold about the world in which we live. In turn, the psychological and physical health of each individual has an impact on how the universe overall evolves. George Bernard Shaw instructs us, "Your purpose in life is simply to help on the purpose of the universe."

How These Beliefs Will Benefit You

When you have a genuine belief in the benevolence of the world, you are able to live your life and go about your daily affairs with a sense of trust that everything will ultimately turn out all right. When things do not go as planned or disaster strikes, it is viewed with a certain amount of detachment and curiosity. Your attitude is one of openness and acceptance that perhaps whatever happened was for an important reason. There is no need to interpret events as catastrophic or as calamities from which you'll never recover.

With a basic trust in life, your orientation is one of good will, a lack of suspicion, and a willingness to take reasonable risks without undue worry and concern over the outcome.

Embracing the world with trust and confidence, it is easier to be more adventurous, open to different ideas and methods, and build your life from inner strengths rather than a hollow shell of ego defenses. There is less fear because, with a basic trust in a larger benevolent universe of which you are a part, what is there to fear? What is there to worry about?

This basic trust gives you a vibrancy, a clearness and spark and persistence that is not possible when you see the world as meaningless, unfriendly and unpredictable.

Belief in an abundant universe implies that "abundance is a given." It is there for the taking. It is not something we need to create in our life, only to allow to come into our life. Whatever we desire is already available. It is simply a matter of claiming it for ourself. There is no shortage or scarcity of resources. Only our beliefs in lack, shortage, poverty and debt bind them to us.

Fears of all those things we don't want in our lives, such as illness, pain or a bad relationship, also have their origin in a lack of trust in the basic goodness of the world.

Events of Your Life

This second cluster of beliefs pertains to how you interpret the circumstances of your life. When things fail to go the way you would like, do you place blame, get upset or find yourself confused? Do you see your days as something to get through, to endure? Over the years, if you've had to face some tough situations before you acquired the mind tools to handle them effectively, you've probably fallen prey to beliefs that left you feeling depressed and full of self-doubts. All of us are subject to lazy, unproductive thinking habits from time to time. To break out of this circular thought trap a number of potent beliefs need to become a regular part of your mind's makeup.

Potent Belief Cluster Two

1. Life is a learning experience, an adventure in time for our growth and expansion. Every so-called failure can be viewed as a learning experience, and as a stepping stone to success. As Thomas Edison said, "I am learning what doesn't work."

2. There is a law of compensation in life that gives us more good things than we ever must endure of the bad. However, we need to recognize and be receptive to its gifts. Richard Bach once said, "There is no such thing as a problem without a gift in its hand."

3. As purposive beings, each of us has a unique mission to fulfill, and we need to interpret the events of our life in the light of that purpose.

Benefits of These Beliefs

When things go wrong, or our experiences seem unfair and unjust, it is viewed as an opportunity to learn something new, to gain an insight or to receive important feedback for change and expansion.

When these success beliefs dominate your thinking, you do not harbor feelings of resentment, blame or anger that life has dealt you a bad hand, or fall into a self-pity party when you find yourself at the bottom of the roller coaster of life. Whatever happens simply is. It is neither judged to be bad or good, but it is seen as an event from which to grow, learn and move on.

You recognize that you do not know the why of everything, that all the information isn't in and probably never will be. Therefore, it's totally up to you to decide how you'll relate to the "missing information" about life. Since giving it a negative spin serves no useful purpose, does nothing to improve your situation and can be seriously costly, you may as well choose other interpretations. After all, that's part of the function of your imagination, to come up with ideas and beliefs that serve you, rather than crucify you. Only you have the power to supervise your mind along empowering channels. No one else.

Direct Your Mind with Power Questions

Thus when you make a mistake, fail or get an unwanted outcome, you direct your mind to ask power questions such as "What can I learn from this situation?" "How else might I interpret these events, other than as being a failure?" "What is going on here that could help me better understand my situation?" "How might I make constructive changes?" "Is there an opportunity I'm missing here?" Grounded in solid, life-enhancing beliefs, these kinds of questions soon become second nature, and you find yourself less and less subject to unfavorable circumstances.

When painful unexplainable experiences do occur and you're prone to cry, "Why me?" lift your mind up and look forward to a positive compensatory gift to offset and more than balance out the downside. Winifred Newman, the noted poet and visionary reminds us, "There are no hopeless situations, only people who think hopelessly." Difficulties are what tell you whether you've got what it takes for real success.

Remember to keep your perspective when things go wrong. Refuse to allow little irritations and troubles disturb you. You are only as big as the things that you worry about. Seek the beauty and splendor of a magnificent life and it will be there for you.

Beliefs About Others

The vast majority of our problems stem from our interpersonal relationships. Much of this difficulty can be traced to the basic beliefs we hold about other people. Many of the beliefs and judgments we make of others are inherited from our culture, our family or media influence. We fall into the habit of thinking about others as we see those around us doing. Because we receive little formal education in how to communicate effectively with others (unless it is for some self-serving purpose), we kind of blunder along, forming our beliefs in a haphazard fashion without a clue as to how they're affecting us.

As discussed earlier, most of our thinking about others is dominated by comparative, quantitative and evaluative thinking. We see others as a package of commodities, of pluses and minuses, based on their educational degrees, racial characteristics, physical appearance, talents and material possessions.

Such beliefs have a tremendous influence on the quality of our lives and everyone around us. The cumulative impact of this obsolete way of thinking about others has led to a multitude of society's ills. Fortunately, we can reverse these destructive tendencies and shift to more constructive ways of relating to one another. Some of the most promising of these are listed below.

Potent Belief Cluster Three

1. *Acceptance.* I accept others without judgment. I believe each person is doing the best he or she is capable of at this point in time. It is foolish and futile for me to judge anyone, regardless of any differing values between us or whether he or she lives up to my expectations. If I wish to influence those who hold opposing values and opinions, I do so in an atmosphere of acceptance, without any tone of disapproval, criticism, blame or bias. I believe it is mutually beneficial to keep an open attitude, free of ego defensiveness.

2. *Trust.* I believe in the basic goodness of each person irrespective of his or her behaviors. I believe that focusing on the best in others brings their best to light and is beneficial to all concerned. I make a conscious effort to do so.

3. *Appreciation of differences.* I believe it makes more sense to view others as simply different rather than making comparisons. Each person has his or her own unique purpose to fulfill, and it is neither necessary nor productive to evaluate him or her using superior—inferior, better than—worse than or other comparative terms.

4. *Shared souls.* All of humanity is interconnected in ways we do not always understand. Each person can be

viewed as an extension of myself. Although the physical bodies we inhabit are separate, we share powerful invisible links. By thinking unkind thoughts of one another or intentionally harming someone, in effect I injure a part of myself. When disputes arise, I think in terms of the resolution of "our needs" rather than "my needs."

5. *Forgiveness.* I believe that I have the power and choice to fully forgive anyone that has wronged me, and to let go of any negative thoughts toward that person. Letting go of any grievances toward another releases and frees us both.

Adopting These Beliefs Will Change Your Life

Relating to others with trust, confident expectancy and giving them the benefit of the doubt, usually results in self-fulfilling prophecy. Powerful expectations for others are a strong magnet for their realization, whether good or bad.

Genuine acceptance of others, regardless of differences, encourages good will. Thought judgments of disapproval and disrespect can be felt by those we come in contact with and has an impact not only on their lives, but permeates the whole fabric of society.

Avoiding comparisons of others on scales of inferior—superior, worse than—better than, and seeking one-upmanship according to a person's appearance, race, possessions, education, skills and other such criteria has the net effect of reducing friction, disharmony, aggression and encourages cooperative, harmonious relationships for everyone.

The least successful people tend to be the most suspicious, blaming and skeptical of others' motives in their interpersonal interactions. While the trusting person may sometimes be taken advantage of, overall his or her life will reap far more rewards and happiness than the person mired in an attitude of skepticism and suspicion. In order to have harmonious relationships, whether between two individuals or two nations, an atmosphere of trust is mandatory. This basic trust in one another has largely broken down in our world today. Until it is rekindled in our hearts and our institutions, we'll continue to see the negative by-products of strife, aggression and violence throughout our society.

> I have believed the best of every man,
> And find that to believe it is enough
> To make a bad man show him at his best,
> Or a good man swing his lantern higher.
> —William Butler Yeats

Beliefs About Yourself

Hundreds of beliefs make up your self-concept. These include beliefs about your appearance, your health, your education, your intelligence, your financial status and all your skills and talents.

For example, you may have a cluster of beliefs that say you are attractive, have beautiful hair, are pleasingly plump, are well-educated, earn a good salary, are a poor tennis player, a careful driver, a critical thinker, a good mother, a responsible person, *ad infinitum*.

Some of the beliefs that form your self-concept are favorable. Some are unfavorable. And others do not matter that much to you one way or the other. Tom may care little whether he has attractive legs, but he may care a great deal about his sexual prowess with women. It may not matter to you that you are a poor tennis player, but you worry about those extra pounds on your thighs.

The sum total of all your beliefs about yourself forms a composite of your self-image. Your self-esteem quotient is the feelings you have about yourself based on the judgments of your various qualities and their importance to you. Self-worth is usually defined as a deeper-level dimension. We are continually told that we are worthy simply by virtue of being alive. The problem is that few people can fully accept this belief about themselves, especially during tough times. And without this belief, feeling good about oneself and feeling deserving under all circumstances is practically impossible. This single powerful belief is the umbrella under which all of your most vital ideas about yourself are contained. A listing of these primary beliefs follows. Some have been mentioned earlier. They are so important to your success and well-being, however, they need to be repeated.

Potent Belief Cluster Four

1. *Unconditional Acceptance.* I believe that it is not to my advantage to define my value as a person in terms of the current conditions of my life. I accept myself completely, regardless of my present financial situation, the way I look or any problems I face.

2. *Director of my fate.* I believe that I am the director of my mind and have a choice about the thought content that enters my mind and what I focus on. I know that my dominant thoughts and beliefs have a powerful impact on the quality of my life.

3. *What I do matters.* I believe that my choices, efforts and actions matter, irrespective of the outcome, that is, whether I receive positive or negative results.

4. *Deserving.* I believe that I am deserving of a prosperous life and good treatment from others.

5. *Purposive.* I believe that I have a reason for being here, even if I am not fully clear about that purpose.

6. *Blameless.* I believe that I am responsible and make the best choices I'm capable of at each moment in time. I refuse to beat myself up for past mistakes or errors.

7. Self-awareness. I believe that I need to stay awake to my choices and their consequences, and expand on the fully aware, conscious direction of my mind and behavior.

All of us, at different periods of our lives, may suffer bouts of lowered self-esteem. As we discussed earlier, to the extent our identities are tied to our careers, financial status, physical appearance and personal relationships, the more insecure we'll find ourselves. We're conditioned to believe that it's somehow our fault when a vital dimension of our life is less than perfect.

The closer your identity is locked into a set of ideal conditions, the more you'll suffer when things go wrong. Since change is a natural part of living, your self-esteem is riding on shaky ground until you have acquired a different perspective about your value and worth as a person.

To have and sustain deep feelings of self-worth, you must believe that you are here for a purpose, that your life has meaning, and that the special circumstances of your life exist for a reason, even when you are unable to ascertain what those reasons might be.

Decide Today to Make These Beliefs into a Regular Part of Your Thinking

Making the decision to begin implanting these potent belief families into your mind and letting them become a regular habit of thinking will have dramatic consequences for your life. As you put the new belief patterns into use, they expand, displacing former limiting patterns. Thomas Blande, the eminent philosopher, reminds us: "In your thoughts today you are building the blueprint of what you will become tomorrow."

Chapter 12
Key Ideas

1. Your life is governed by a complex network of belief clusters. Four primary belief families are: your worldview; beliefs about the events in your life; beliefs about others; and beliefs about yourself.

2. The beliefs you hold in these areas have profound consequences for your happiness and well-being.

3. You have the power to add, delete and revise the thoughts and beliefs housed in your mind's compartments.

4. Selecting those potent belief clusters that positively impact your life is your right and choice to make.

5. Former faulty belief patterns fall away as you adopt and expand on new high-potency beliefs and make them a regular part of your thinking habits.

"Remember happiness doesn't depend upon who you are or what you have; it depends solely upon what you think."
—Dale Carnegie

IV
AGENDA FOR CHANGE

"The world we have made as a result of the level of thinking we have done thus far creates problems we cannot solve at the same level at which we created them."
—Albert Einstein

Chapter 13

Five Star Thinking
Your Sphere of Choice

"The greatest undeveloped asset in the world today is man's thinking. Surely it is up to us to at least get our own thinking on the right basis. No one else can do it for us."
—William Ross

Changing Old Belief Patterns

Up to this point we have emphasized the importance of the thoughts and beliefs you hold in your mind. You have learned that your dominant thoughts and beliefs determine your experiences, that what you think about constantly soon becomes manifest in your life. You have also learned that you have the power to choose and change the content of your mind, to add new beliefs, reshape old ones and displace those that are having an adverse effect on your life.

But how do you go about doing this? How do you change long-entrenched belief patterns? What is the process by which these changes take place? It is easy to understand that having a solid belief in yourself and your capabilities under all circumstances would be valuable to your life. But if you do not always feel capable and worthy, how can you arrive at a point in your mind where you have a genuine and deep conviction that you are? You can be positive and declare that we live in a purposive, benevolent universe, but if an inner cynical voice raises doubts in your mind, where do you go from there? We can say the words; we can repeat affirmations, but until we are definitely convinced of the validity of our new beliefs, they will carry little weight in our lives.

In a moment I'll be giving you steps that will assist you in this change process. First, we need to back up and lay the groundwork. Before constructive change can occur consistently you need to have a basic understanding of how your mind operates. Change is always taking place; we're just not usually directing it for our benefit. For the most part, we've been discussing the content of your mind, that is, your thoughts and beliefs. Now we need to look at you, the person behind this content, and the ways in which you think.

Your Mode of Thinking

How do you typically define life's events? How do you interpret your successes and failures? Your daily perceptions and interpretations of life's situations and events become your beliefs. If you pronounce yourself a failure every time something goes wrong, you'll soon have a battery of self-defeating beliefs. Along with this if you tend to interpret your successes as "guess I just got lucky" instead of giving yourself credit, you're building beliefs in chance, luck and fate.

You are the person in charge of your beliefs and your mind's content. You have the inner power to call life as you choose. And as you do, you move beyond the realm of chance and into the mind's power of influence. You actually begin shaping events. I'm sure you've heard the expression, "It's all in the eyes of the beholder." The ways in which you perceive, define, and interpret life's experiences is in your hands. This is what psychologists refer to as your cognitive mode—your characteristic style of thinking. Psychologists have identified a variety of these modes of thinking. Some attract success and enrich your life. Others breed failure, flawed beliefs, and personal bankruptcy. Modes of thinking are learned and can be changed.

Five Star Thinking

Five Star Thinking is a powerful mode that will enhance every aspect of your life and propel you toward greater personal and financial success.

Five Star Thinkers define life from a higher plane. Where others see impossibility, they see possibilities for change and personal growth. Five Star Thinkers act out of a sphere of clear awareness, free from the bias of past negative conditioning. When things go wrong, when one gets rejected or Murphy's Law strikes, it is not taken personally. Problems are viewed as temporary setbacks, in the past, over and done with, as a chance to learn and move on.

Five Star Thinkers both view and define events in a way that influences outcomes in their favor. Mistakes and failures are seen as stepping stones to success. The uncertainties of life never get the best of them because they're soaring above them. Their egos are not stuck in the muck of self-doubts, despair or defensive tactics. With the wings of Five Star Thinking they see beyond their problems and the day-to-day downers. They soar in the rich potential of the mind that the majority of folks have never tapped into—that great ninety percent of unused potential we hear so much about.

Five Star Thinkers are convinced of their worthiness, their value, and their capabilities in spite of any mistakes, human errors or failures.

Five Star Thinkers see opportunities and adventures everywhere. They are void of gloom and doom, woe-is-me thinking. Instead of problems, the Five Star Thinker sees challenge. Five Star Thinkers are creative—seeing a way around, over or through every obstacle that comes along.

Five Star Thinking is studded with success beliefs—beliefs that radiate and attract riches, love and rewards.

How can you begin putting this revolutionary new mode of thinking into practice in your life? First you need to know how your mind works.

How Your Mind Works

As complex and miraculous as our mind is, it is governed by some very simple psychological laws. When you understand how these laws operate, you will be able to work with them rather than letting them randomly rule your life.

As we saw previously, very early in our development, our mind begins generating impressions and ideas about the self, life and events. These ideas come to us from our social environment—our family, neighbors, the media and the culture we grow up in. Our mind learns to reason or think using these ideas and impressions that we've formed. It is out of these ideas that we make decisions and act.

Now many of these ideas about ourselves, others and life are in error or only partially true, but we fail to see them as such insofar as we're trapped within their context. That is, we can only think with the data or information that we have in our mind. Over time many of these early formulated ideas take the form of opinions and beliefs. Now they have taken on a power of their own. As an idea becomes a deeply-held conviction or belief, it generates strong emotions and feelings. For example, if we believe someone has done us an injustice, whether we're right or wrong, we're going to *feel* angry and upset. If we formed an early impression of ourselves as being inferior in some way and so far this has been borne out by our experiences (we now believe it), then we're going to *feel* the emptiness, despair and self-doubts of inferiority. That's simply the way our mind works. Beliefs produce feelings and emotions. And the stronger the belief, the stronger the feelings associated with it. Feelings, in turn, trigger actions which can either impede or aid your success.

Like it or not, for better or for worse, our beliefs are running our lives. The way out of this is not through more rational or logical thinking because we can only think within the context of the beliefs, impressions and ideas we currently hold. The way to freedom is to go beyond them...to take a mental step into the sphere of conscious awareness that engulfs your mind's content. This is not some hocus pocus mental process. It's a simple choice that you can make and do.

To escape from negative and self-defeating beliefs, we need to step into our sphere of choice. As humans, each of us has a sphere of conscious awareness, of choice and free will. It is here that you are the creator, the orchastrator and director of your mind's content and activities. It is in this realm of being that you become the master of your fate.

View Your Beliefs as Hypotheses

To move into this sphere of choice and Five Star Thinking, you need to let go of the notion that your beliefs are you. Your beliefs are not who you are. They are simply mind tools for you—the real you—to use. Start viewing your beliefs as hypotheses, i.e., tentative ideas that have an impact on your life. Unlike beliefs or solid convictions, hypotheses are always tentative and subject to change. Our ideas are continually tested in experience; we receive feedback and based on how we interpret this feedback, we revise, delete and form new ideas. Many of these ideas then become our beliefs.

I want you to begin viewing all the personal beliefs you hold as tentative ideas. Your beliefs are not set in cement. They are fluid dynamic structures.

The problem is that we have come to view our beliefs as facts, as established truths, and we live our lives as if this were the case. If you believe yourself to be unattractive, you act according to this belief and are subject to the consequences. If you believe that you are inferior and undeserving, you have a set of expectations that soon become a self-fulfilling prophecy. If you are convinced people are not to be trusted, this belief will be reflected in your social interactions. If you believe the universe is unpredictable, random and arbitrary, your life is likely to be filled with cynicism and fear.

"But," you insist, "what if the bulk of my experiences, the evidence of my senses and my perceptions of reality do not support the positive beliefs about myself, others and the world that you are suggesting I subscribe to?"

How well your beliefs fit the facts of life as you currently know them is not a very useful way of thinking because your particular "fact-fit" is always limited to your slice of the pie of past experiences; you always see only a small portion of total reality. And our so-called facts shift and change as new information comes to light. This is why we have a world filled with diverse beliefs and opinions. We find little consensus on anything—whether it be religion, politics, educational practices or family structures.

Allow for Missing Information
Using Five Star Thinking, you regard your facts as tentative and keep an opening in your mind for the information that isn't in yet, that you haven't been exposed to, experienced, or discovered. Without this opening you not only are stuck with whatever beliefs you happen to have at the

moment irrespective of new information coming to light (you won't see it), but you also will be unable to experience growth and learning.

The wider this opening in your mind's eye, the greater is your ability to expand, see clearly, take a larger view and move toward each of your goals in harmony. Without this, you will continually be bumping heads with those who hold different ideas. And to the extent that your ego and identity is set in these beliefs, you'll feel threatened and frustrated. For when you see yourself only in terms of the beliefs you hold, then when they are criticized or attacked, that is, you bump up against opposing views, you will feel threatened.

Strong Beliefs Generate Strong Emotions

And the greater the intensity of the belief, the stronger the emotion associated with it, and the greater the threat. If you see yourself as having no identity or self outside of your belief systems, then the threat is very personal. It is *you* who is being attacked. You feel your very life is at stake. Small wonder we go to war, maiming and killing those who have differences from us. We feel threatened. We feel we must preserve ourselves and those like us, that is, who share our beliefs.

Resolving Inner Conflicts

The conflict can also be an inner one, since we all hold beliefs that contradict others held in our mind. This is a normal state because information is always in flux, as are the mental structures we form to hold it together in some kind of meaningful whole. Understanding the basic ways that change occurs and how beliefs are formed, we no longer are confused or disturbed by these disparities. Without this understanding we typically fall back on Grade D modes of thinking, shutting out new ideas while protecting and defending our existing beliefs, whether they are hurting us or helping us.

Fortunately, it is neither necessary nor advantageous to retain only those personal beliefs that fit-the-facts as you currently know them. You can expand your mind to always include the "missing link," the missing information, the gap that always exists, no matter how much knowledge you have at your disposal. For as soon as we acquire one set of facts, new unknowns crop up. The element of uncertainty is, paradoxically, a given.

What you are doing is simply making a provision in your mind for the missing or unknown data. You are allowing for the facts that aren't in yet. You are making an opening for the potential of what could be, if it isn't. William James, noted Harvard psychologist and philosopher, instructs us to "act as if" something is so, and it will become so. Adopting the powerful success beliefs that benefit you makes good sense, irrespective of your perceptions of their current truth. The yardstick is their usefulness and effect on your life. Leland Kaiser once said, "Don't worry about predicting the future. Create it."

You—As Observer

With Five Star Thinking, you stand over your present pattern of beliefs and are in a position to reshape them according to the dictates of your goals and desires. From this new heightened stance you become a keen observer of the impact of your beliefs on your experiences. You are able to actually begin seeing the cause—effect links. Working within the laws of psychology, *you* become the cause agent—using the tools of your mind to produce the results you desire. When you become mentally adept at stepping back from your beliefs and looking out over them objectively with no ego ties, you are able to fashion them in your best interests.

Freedom from Destructive Emotional Reactions

This remarkable stance also allows you to move beyond self-defeating reactions provoked by cruel treatment from others or harsh situations. From your new vantage point, you are in a position to choose a more appropriate response, thought or emotion than the one triggered by the event. If someone makes an unkind remark, and anger has been your predominant response in the past, once you have the Five Star habit, you can step back from this emotion and make your own choices about what you'd like your response to be. You can select whatever behaviors are consistent with your values and serve the larger picture of your life.

Five Star Thinking keeps you free from the interference of emotionally-charged beliefs already existing in your mind, defusing their negative effect as you attend to your daily affairs. It "lets in" those mighty belief clusters that have the power for running your life along more promising and prosperous channels.

Five Star Thinking leaves us open to the possibility of ideas that have not yet entered our imaginations, wisdom that is but a wisp in our mind, and potentials that remain invisible to our senses. Freeing up our identity from a rigid mold of flawed beliefs, Five Star Thinking embraces not just a new set of beliefs or ideas but a different way of thinking about all our beliefs and experiences.

Five Star Thinking—A Powerful Mind Strategy

Five Star Thinking, then, represents a powerful mind vehicle for forming ideas from the broader perspective of your overall needs and desires. Your acceptance or rejection of any personal beliefs is based strictly on the kind of impact they'll have on your life. Do they further a happier, more harmonious and successful life or not?

From this stance you take reality into your hands, changing and shaping it into positive outcomes. You are the creator and molder of your fate. Your tools are your thoughts and beliefs.

Taking Charge of Your Great Potential

Adopting the Five Star posture, with its provision for incomplete information, you are now in a position to make use of your full potential. Within your sphere of choice, you can mentally guide this potential for movement in the direction of desired change, that is, you can deliberately and decisively influence the course of events. We all do this to a certain extent, but mostly it's been through trial-and-error methods with only minimal awareness of how the mind—event process works.

Five Star Thinking releases you from the heavy baggage of past mistakes, failures and all the toxic emotions that go along with them—guilt, shame and pain. You also become free of fear and the whole emotional bundle springing from fear—anger, resentment, jealousy, self-doubt and despair. You need never again be besieged by these negative, unproductive emotions. When an event in your life acts to trigger anxiety, insecurity or fear, all you need do is remind yourself that you have the power to mentally step into your sphere of choice and take control of the situation. Yes, it takes practice. Learning new mental skills is just like learning any other task. As a child we didn't learn how to ride a bicycle on the first try. However, please don't make the mistake of underestimating the power of this new way of thinking because of its simplicity.

Nor am I saying that you'll never feel anger or anxiety again. It's perfectly okay and normal to feel these emotions occasionally. They're part of the human condition. You don't however want your life run by these feelings. And you certainly do not want depression, self-doubts and despair interfering with your important goals and dreams for the future. Nor do you want your fears to stand in the way of the success you deserve. Just telling yourself to stop being afraid or unhappy or angry doesn't cut it. Most of us know what we should do. We just don't know how. When you understand how your mind works and how emotions originate, then you have the power and freedom to release them.

Within your sphere of choice, you are the creator of your beliefs and thoughts, and thereby your emotions and feelings. You are the director of your destiny. You are the artist that is painting the landscape and scenes of your life.

Most importantly, the Five Star strategy allows for the self that exists beyond your beliefs and life's uncertainties. This permits you to consciously navigate within your mighty potential toward the vision of what can be without being stranded and trapped in your mind's past and present "factory" of what is.

Chapter 13
Key Ideas

1. Five Star Thinking is a mind strategy anyone can learn to use with practice. It represents a different way of thinking about your experiences and the beliefs you hold. Key characteristics include the following:

   A. Beliefs are viewed as hypotheses (tentative ideas) rather than irrefutable facts.
   B. New beliefs are selected based on how well they test out in experience, eliciting desired events.
   C. You are able to accept beliefs into your mind whether or not they presently appear true because of your allowance for the incompleteness of information.
   D. Taking this information gap into account permits you to stamp out those beliefs thwarting your success, and adopt those beliefs that build riches.
   E. It also opens up a powerful influence factor in your mind that lets you shape the course of events.

2. Putting Five Star Thinking into practice in your daily affairs will revolutionize your life.

"The way we think determines how we live"
—John Miller

Chapter 14

Steps for Building Success Beliefs

"It's not who you know;
It's not what you know
It's what you believe."
—Author

Congratulations! You've come a long way. Now you are going to learn exactly how to make success beliefs a permanent part of your life. To enter new beliefs into your thinking and eject flawed ones, three things need to happen: one, you need to be *receptive* to the new belief; two, it has to *register* in your mind; and three, you must be able to easily *recall* it. These three R's are clarified below.

Three Prerequisites for Belief Change to Occur
1. You need to be receptive to the new belief.
There has to be a willingness on your part to allow the new information in without the resistance of a host of ifs, ands or buts. "Oh, but I'm not that smart or talented or capable." The new belief needs to penetrate your current self-limiting thought structures and be welcomed into your mind

even if perceived as an alien visitor that does not readily fit in with the rest of your beliefs and ideas.

The closer it is to your current beliefs, the easier it will be to accept. The challenge is to create an opening for those beliefs that do not currently support the facts.

As complex human beings, many of our ideas are contradictory and at arms with one another. The secret to coming to peace with this cohabitation of opposing beliefs is to just allow them to be. Don't forget; you are the creator of your thoughts and beliefs. You have the power to put whatever you choose into your mind. Your mind's storehouse of beliefs represents a giant potpourri of tools for your benefit. It is up to you to add new belief ingredients and throw out old disruptive patterns as you see fit based on the consequences they hold for your life.

2. The new belief has to register in your mind.

Once you have mentally prepared yourself for the acceptance of a new belief, the idea has to register in your mind. That is, you need to *make the decision* to accept it without any reservations. I guarantee you can learn to do this with practice in spite of the ifs, ands or buts that come up. Shortly, you'll be given specific steps for reinforcing this decision.

Your goal is to accumulate a supply of high-grade success beliefs that apply to the different dimensions of your life: your views about yourself, others, events, important concerns and the world. In other words, you are mentally taking in and imprinting empowering beliefs into your mind's structure. Remember, you can't think with beliefs and thoughts that don't even exist in your mind.

3. You must be able to recall the new belief when you need it.

For new beliefs to be useful to you, they must be retained and readily accessible. Our natural tendency to is respond from old belief patterns.

Let's say that when you make a mistake, you are in the habit of voicing to yourself: "I can't do anything right. There must be something wrong with me. I'm never going to amount to anything."

To reverse this tendency, you'll need to remind yourself that these are just thoughts, not facts—old belief patterns that you have the power to dismiss. You quickly shift your focus to your new beliefs. You want the new success belief cluster to be right on the tip of your tongue, ready to replace the old, damaging belief habits.

As complex and intricate as the brain is, when you definitely decide to take the helm and consciously begin directing your mighty belief tools, you'll be happily surprised to discover how easily everything falls into place.

In sum, you need to mentally open the door to the new belief, let it in, and be able to grab hold of it when you need it.

Specific Steps for Building New Beliefs

Now that you have laid the groundwork, installing your new success beliefs is a simple, one-two-three process.

First, you need to decide which success beliefs to select for your initial installation process (New Belief Affirmation).

Second, give yourself specific reasons for the new beliefs (Development of Personal Convincers).

And third, take the appropriate action steps to support and reinforce the new beliefs (Supportive Action Steps).

Step 1
New Belief Affirmation

We begin by selecting those high potency beliefs that will have the greatest overall positive effect on your life. That is, which beliefs will have the most dramatic impact on your financial status, career, relationships and health?

While this varies from person to person depending on their present situation, we'll start off with a belief cluster that has had a high success rate for virtually everyone.

In the last chapter we identified high potency beliefs in several areas: how you view the world and events, beliefs about others, and most importantly, the beliefs you hold about yourself.

A powerful belief triad for massive success is comprised of three beliefs that we've been emphasizing all along:

1. I am a worthy person.
2. I deserve success.
3. What I do matters.

Once these beliefs become definitely accepted by your mind, you'll immediately begin experiencing positive results. Self doubts and fears will vanish. You'll be able to handle whatever situations arise.

In this first step you are simply to affirm verbally and in written form: "I am a worthy person who deserves success. What I do matters." This is a powerful idea. Say it out loud and write it down in the space below. If contradictory or negative thoughts surface, don't try to resist them, just let them be. It's okay to allow opposing ideas to exist side by side. The old self-destructive beliefs will fall away of their own accord as you do these exercises.

Remind yourself again that your beliefs and thoughts, though invisible, are dynamic, malleable tools obedient to your directions. You have the power to focus on whatever beliefs you choose, and right now you choose to give your attention to the idea that you are a worthy, deserving person whose actions matter. Past behaviors, events, failures and mistakes have no bearing. At this special moment in time, you have stepped within your sphere of choice and Five Star Thinking to supervise your beliefs for your benefit and good.

Step 2
Development of Personal Convincers

The second step involves mindstorming for reasons that you personally find convincing in accepting the new beliefs.

Give yourself compelling reasons for holding this belief cluster. I'm going to offer a few suggestions for you to use as a starting point and a springboard to your own imagination. You are to mindstorm until you find convincers that wedge an opening in your mind, however slight that opening might be. Tailor your reasonings as best you can to sway and capture your own logical thinking and persuasion.

In some instances this is accomplished merely by raising doubts about existing unproductive thoughts.

Here are some thought fragments to begin with for building self worth:

"I was born. I can believe it was an accident, a cruel joke or I can think of it in more positive terms. The choice is mine. I choose to believe I am worthy and deserving because I am here. I was born as a unique person and I choose to give myself the benefit of the doubt that my life has merit and value. I would apply that logic to my children, why not to myself?"

"Even though I may not know explicitly why or how my life has meaning, I have the free will and power to adopt this belief about myself."

"Being worthy and deserving are, after all, value judgments that are relative to changing norms and ideas. I do not need to define my worth as a person in terms of my financial or occupational status, prestigious positions, celebrity status, awards, good looks or any other such standards."

"I am important enough to have landed on this strange earth land. If indeed I am a spiritual being with a temporary body to inhabit, the amount of money, houses, cars, and gadgets I own doesn't carry much weight from the perspective of eternity. Nor does holding a high status position, or even being president of a company or country."

"And if I'm a soul with a body, I surely came here for a reason. At least I know I can entertain the idea. That has to be evidence for something."

"Other people's opinions about me do not need to carry much weight in my mind. What do they know? I have my own mind to think about myself and find it totally unnecessary to take-in or be-taken-in by anyone else's unfriendly thoughts about me."

"When I really think about it, the most important thing about me would seem to be the remarkable human aspect of having a creative imagination and a profound self awareness, being able to know myself and my mind's activities. Although it's something we all have and take for granted, like the air we breathe, when I reflect on it, it's quite astonishing. The fact that these features are not unique to me does not lessen their value. Actually it is just the opposite. Who decreed that I must distinguish myself in some way from others to have value? My self-worth can just as easily lie in similar features rather than differences. I can hang my worthiness on anything I choose."

Some of these convincers will sound plausible to you. Others won't. The basic idea with this exercise is less in the arguments than the strategy behind them—the flexible style of thinking that you use. Your mindstorming search is for possibilities—explanations that allow you to entertain more viable beliefs about yourself than all the self-defeating thought crust you have accumulated over the years.

You are attempting to wedge an opening in your mind free from bias, judgment and rejection of the new beliefs. Use your imagination and convince yourself once and for all that you are truly a worthy, deserving person, and that your actions matter.

Step 3
Supportive Action

It is time to begin taking specific action steps to reinforce your new beliefs. Your beliefs do not exist in a vacuum nor are they divorced from your actions. There is a continual back-and-forth process for belief reinforcement. Therefore, you not only need to take the mental steps for mind change to occur, but must perform the actions that support those changes.

You want to begin deliberately acting out your new beliefs, i.e., taking actions that are consistent with your new battery of beliefs. You are to walk your talk.

What specific behaviors demonstrate "I am a worthy deserving person, and what I do matters?" What action steps will move you in the direction of these new beliefs?

A host of behaviors follow from this powerful belief triad. They include how you treat yourself, what you say and do in relation to others, and how you handle various business functions. In short, the whole gamut of your activities is affected.

As you become comfortable with the new belief triad in your mind and you habitually fall back on the self-reflection "I am a worthy, deserving person and what I do matters," all actions that are consistent with this belief set will follow automatically. For now, however, a conscious intervention effort is required. You are to identify specific actions you can take *this week* that support and reinforce the belief. Listed below are six possibilities. Select at least three of these that you *definitely* will follow through on. Each small action step you take will strengthen your new beliefs and enrich your life.

1. Treat my body as if it is important with (A)regular exercise and (B)a good diet.

A. A minimum of twenty minutes a day, four times per week is suggested in the physical activity of your choice, whether walking, jogging, biking, stair steps or yoga.

B. If you're not giving yourself a regular diet of healthy foods, decide on one healthy food you've been neglecting (for example, a fruit or vegetable) and add it to your diet this week.

2. Be kind to myself verbally.

Say nice things to yourself, at least once a day for the coming week. Compliment yourself on everything you do or have done well in the past.

3. Reward myself after completion of a task.

Give yourself a gift, bonus, trip, night out or something you've been wanting after completion of a project or goal. If you are working on long-term goals, reward yourself incrementally when you reach a quarter, or halfway point. You are a worthy, deserving person. Treat yourself like one.

4. Seek out growth and learning experiences.

People who feel important and worthy continually seek to improve themselves. Select one of the items listed below to begin this week.

A. Decide on a new skill you'd like to develop and set up a plan for it.

B. Take a class on something you've been wanting to learn about, such as art, photography or a computer language.

C. Make reservations for a conference in a field of interest, e.g., education, sewing, creative writing, or arts and crafts.

D. Enroll in local music or dance classes.

E. Go to the library or bookstore and obtain a book or tape on self-improvement.

5. *Speak to others as if I am an important, worthy person.*

Specifically, commit to one of the following activities:

A. Express appreciation to a friend or acquaintance for something they've done for you or just for who they are.

B. Say kind words and give support to someone down in the dumps at least two times over the next week. Start today.

C. Pay a sincere compliment to a service person (a grocery clerk, taxi driver or waitress).

People with strong feelings of self-worth and esteem treat others with kindness and respect. Secure in their own skin, they genuinely care about the welfare of other people and this is reflected in their attitudes and behaviors. Small acts of kindness, consideration, expressions of appreciation and offering support when appropriate are natural outcomes of a solid belief in one's self-worth.

Those who have fully come to terms with who they are— worthy and important in their own right—have no interest in diminishing others with verbal abuse of blaming, complaining or berating, much less with malicious gossip, or anger. There is simply no place in their mind for the flawed personal deficit beliefs that spark such destructive behaviors.

6. *Demonstrate self-acceptance in the face of mistakes.*

Probably more than any other behavior, those with deep feelings of self-worth and self-respect, treat themselves well in the face of failure, mistakes and shortcomings. Instead of beating themselves up with self-reprisals for what they did wrong, they stand back, appraise the situation objectively and seek improvement next time.

Think back over your past and identify an instance where you berated yourself and have felt guilt or shame. Redefine the situation from your new image and upgraded beliefs of self-worth and self-respect. Pat yourself on the back for your efforts and the fact that you did the best you knew how at the time. Confirm to yourself self-acceptance and the dismissal of any lingering defeatist feelings by treating yourself to a day of leisure—doing something fun just for making the decision to let go of damaging beliefs and emotions.

From Chance Happenings to Taking Charge

These three steps parallel the ways in which your beliefs have been formed and shaped throughout your life. That is, you make observations and form ideas. You mentally test them out (reason whether or not they make sense for you to accept). And you act them out in your experiences, receiving feedback from which you make corrections or formulate new ideas.

All this takes place, for the most part, without benefit of our awareness, approval and intervention. Our mind's storehouse of beliefs has been built from our parent's and teacher's views, our culture's biases and the early experiences we have happened into. Yes, we made choices, but these were always the product of our current stock of beliefs. No one taught us how our ideas and beliefs were formed, and how we can change them and improve our lives.

What you have learned to do now is take active control over this process. Instead of randomly, subconsciously accepting beliefs about yourself and life, you are bringing the process within your sphere of choice—under the direction and supervision of your own management. You are making choices about the beliefs and thoughts which you *want* to dwell in your mind, based on how they play out in your life.

You have just taken the most important steps you will ever take to insure your success and happiness. Regular practice will result in permanent and abundant rewards. Apply these simple steps to other success belief clusters to accelerate the change process. A list of eleven empowering belief triads is given in the appendix. Make each of these an automatic part of your thinking and reap the benefits!

Chapter 14
Key Ideas

1. For belief change to occur, you need to take into account the three R's of learning: Receptivity, Registration and Recall. You need to be receptive to the new belief. Its meaning must register in your mind. And you have to be able to easily recall the new belief.

2. There is a continual back-and-forth feedback cycle between your mind and the experiences out of which your beliefs are formed. For belief change to occur in the desired direction, you must consciously take charge of this cycle.

3. Building success beliefs is accomplished via three easy steps: Affirm your new beliefs. Give yourself personal convincers for the new beliefs. Take action steps to reinforce the new beliefs.

4. Installing success beliefs is an ongoing process that is accelerated and sustained through consistent, regular practice.

5. Your experiences can only be as rich and rewarding as the beliefs you adopt and put into action. Major changes come about in your life through these simple, easy steps. You need only make the choice and begin today.

"First we think, then we act. To consciously think that we 'can' impels the subconscious faculties into action."
—Walter Matthews

V
PERSONAL CATALYSTS

"He does not believe that does not live according to his belief."
—Thomas Fuller

Chapter 15

Belief Boosters

"Believe you have it, and you have it."
—Latin Proverb

You are now prepared to fully meet life's challenges, and reap its rich treasures. In this final chapter are seven reminders to ensure the ongoing mastery of your mind's great powers for your success and happiness. It is recommended that you refer back to these ideas frequently. Make them a part of your thinking and habit patterns. Allow them to enrich and enhance your journey through life.

1. Your Life Has Purpose and Meaning.

You are a person with a purpose in life, whether or not you have discovered just what that purpose is. Pay attention to the strong creative impulse that tugs at your innermost being. A deep desire to do something, a compelling sense of urgency is generally related to your unique purpose. By surrendering to it, you give meaning to your life. Ignoring or suppressing this urging is detrimental to both your mental and physical health.

Live according to this purpose. It is an umbrella under which everything else in your life falls into place. Maintain your vision, taking one goal at a time. You are in the pilot's seat and the director of your fate. Put yourself in charge of your beliefs and thoughts and maintain obedience to your best self.

Ask for what you want in life and believe that it is there for you. If you don't know something, search for it. If you need something, look for it. Move toward your desires and wishes. Steadily held beliefs will take you where you want to go.

Every effort counts regardless of the outcome. Every action taken with right intention in the direction of your goals matters. Each time you make a decision and follow through on it, you build inner strength, irrespective of any temporary setbacks, mistakes or disappointing results. Know this is so and remind yourself that what you're doing matters, even when all does not turn out as you wished.

Think: "Consistent, concerted effort."

Every small step counts. Settle this once and for all with yourself, because each small step you take has a ripple effect on your life that is much larger.

Think: "I am destined to be great—great in my own way. It is my inherent right."

2. Stay Focused on High-Potency Beliefs.

Whatever you focus your attention upon continually will become manifest in your life. Your dominant thoughts and beliefs determine your destiny. You can learn to shift your focus from one belief to another. You have the ability to take the best of your beliefs and put those in charge, in a position of power, before making a decision or taking action. Remind yourself that you are always at liberty to focus on whatever belief you choose. When an old, faulty belief surfaces in your mind, you can switch your mind over to a newly-installed, upgraded one. You develop competency in this area with practice and by stepping into your sphere of choice on a regular basis.

Those conditions you think about constantly will expand in your life. Show appreciation for what you have and what you'd like to happen. Give your attention to the results you want. Orison Swett Marden, the renowned philosopher, tells us, "What we think most about is constantly weaving itself into the fabric of our career, becoming a part of ourselves, increasing the power of our mental magnet to attract those things which we most ardently desire."

Thoughts of all persuasions pass through our minds. Yet the thoughts and beliefs we grab hold of and dwell on at length are what determine the fate of our lives. It is probably correct to say that you are not responsible for the thoughts that sporadically happen into your inner world, but that you are very much responsible for those thoughts you cling to and nurture. These will color and create your mental imagery and finally become a part of your world, determining what you attract into your life.

When negative, damaging beliefs surface, shove them in the closet of your mind and bolt the door. They can have no effect unless activated, that is, focused and dwelled upon by you. When you install their opposites in your mind and keep them activated, the old faulty patterns will fade away for lack of attention, finally dying out completely. Use your inner voice of authority and declare the seniority of your success belief clusters.

You have absolute dominion over your thoughts and beliefs. Within your sphere of choice, you can decide to accept a particular belief, irrespective of the circumstances of your life or your existing package of beliefs. You might think of beliefs as airplanes. You can allow a belief to land in your mind and stay there, or you can instruct it to fly away.

Remember, your beliefs are not carved in stone but are made of clay and can be consciously molded as you choose.

3. Be Clear About the Impact and Positive Potential of Your Beliefs.

The quality of your life will be only as good as the quality of your beliefs and thoughts. As you begin to see the changes in your experiences from adopting high potency beliefs, your enthusiasm and energy will skyrocket. Empowering beliefs can revitalize energy, trigger positive action when you're in a slump, keep you on target and lend direction to your life. Grade A beliefs help break cycles of self-recrimination, blame, resentment and anger.

To gain full mastery of the beliefs and thoughts dwelling in your mind is to gain mastery of your life. The degree to which you perfect your skills here will be the degree to which life with all its treasures opens its doors for you.

4. Loosen Your Attachment to Faulty Beliefs.

We fall in love with our beliefs. Not only those positive beliefs that bolster us and are good for us but we cling to those beliefs that are preventing us from the achievement of important goals. They become locked into our identity, who and what we believe ourselves to be. And we generally reinforce them by seeking out people, books, groups and social affiliations that support and confirm our existing beliefs.

Let go of beliefs that aren't serving your best interests by learning to loosen this attachment. Step back from your box of beliefs and see them for what they are: fluid thought forms, mind tools for your use and pleasure. Although often hidden, you can learn to bring them out into the open mentally and view them as separate from yourself and who you are.

5. You Are Not Your Beliefs.

Your beliefs have evolved to help you explain life and have a means for making decisions and taking action. No matter how scant our information, we are prone to invent beliefs to explain our world, to help us understand what is happening and why. Beliefs have survival value for our species; however, many of the beliefs we hold are putting our survival and the quality of that survival at high risk.

Begin to think of your beliefs as simply a faculty of mind like your arms and hands are a physical faculty. The mind and its contents are a mental faculty for your use. As a fork and spoon or chopsticks serve us food, so our mental faculties can be refined and serve us better or remain crude like the caveman tools and only minimally serve us.

We tend to confuse this mind faculty with ourselves—who we are. Typically we believe that our thoughts, physical body and emotions are the real us. But who do you suppose is directing the movements of your body, your thoughts and your emotions?

And what do you suppose it is in-between you and your body, thoughts and emotions that is making the connection with others, that is, communicating? It is decidedly something more than articulations of speech or the written word.

There is a self, a sphere of choice surrounding your beliefs that has the freedom to replace and redirect them. This is the real you. This same self has the freedom of choice from the outflow of sentiments and emotions that spring from these beliefs. The anger that erupts from the belief that someone has mistreated you can be released the moment you step back from this Grade D belief into Five Star Thinking. In that split-second pause of awareness and moment of freedom you can let the destructive belief go and replace it with another belief or set of beliefs.

When someone treats you unfairly or is cruel, tell yourself, "People who are unkind to others often have a lot of pain inside them. His actions toward me have nothing to do with my value as a person, and there's no point in letting it interfere with my day." Maybe he is just having a bad day. This doesn't mean you approve of their bad behavior. You're simply making the choice to interpret it in a way that minimizes its negative impact on you. Why give anyone the power to make you angry, upset or depressed?

In the face of a defeat, tell yourself, "I'm disappointed. Nonetheless, there's probably something important I can learn from this experience. Next time I'll do better. It's no reflection on me as a person. I am more than my behaviors or any mistakes which I make." Again, why let any situation or condition get you down and interfere with your desires and dreams? The power is with you, not the situation. It is what it is. You can call it as you choose.

As we have seen, the key is having a storehouse of Grade A beliefs available, for instant recall, ready to replace flawed patterns and to practice their use in real life situations.

When you have made high potency beliefs a part of your mind's repertoire, and learned to use Five Star Thinking, you need never again be under the influence of faulty, destructive beliefs, nor subject to their negative consequences.

6. Strive to Maintain the Open Awareness of Five Star Thinking.

Maintain a clear awareness—open, receptive and sensitive to what's going on around you. Learn to step back from the content of your mind, your beliefs and thoughts, to see lucidly without the interference of past conditioning or any anxiety about the future. Strive for the posture of mind that is uncontaminated by the biases and prejudices inadvertently picked up along the path of living. The more you can live your life from the realm of conscious choice, the greater will be your growth and evolution in harmony with the universe.

Allow for the possibility of new beliefs that do not currently fit-the-facts of your previous experiences or perceptions. Welcome those beliefs that keep you on purpose, living your hopes and dreams.

The formation of your beliefs and thought patterns has been a long gradual process. Changes too will typically be gradual. Learning to reconstruct a head of clouded reality into a more sunny reality isn't likely to happen overnight. But consistent, small mind steps reap big results. You can accelerate these changes by staying on top of the content of your mind. You're looking for permanent, continuous changes in the direction of improved living. Once you begin to develop the dynamic rhythm of this process, you'll find it fun, exciting and pleasantly challenging. It is foremost a journey along the magnificent pathway of life.

7. Get in the Habit of Mentally Testing the Consequences of Your Beliefs and Thoughts.

When a belief or thought comes to mind, ask yourself, "Will this belief lead to the results I desire?" "Will this cluster of beliefs lead to those things I want in life: self-fulfillment, creative expression, financial independence and good relationships?"

"Or will this belief act to inhibit and thwart my hopes and dreams?" If so, then it does not deserve a place in your mind. Why continue to hang on to beliefs that threaten your happiness and enjoyment of life? Why give a standing invitation to thoughts that are clearly jeopardizing your well-being?

Step into your sphere of choice and scrutinize your beliefs in the light of whether they're expanding your growth and development. Examine them through the lens of whether they're making your stay on earth a happy, harmonious place to be or one of struggle and hardship and pain. If they fall into the latter group, it's time to toss them into the dumpster. Your beliefs are a tool for living the good life. Treat your beliefs as if your life depended on them, because it does.

It is imprudent and irresponsible to retain thought and belief baggage that is keeping us at war with our neighbors, that is restricting our growth and productivity or hindering the accomplishment of worthy goals and dreams. As you become more aware of yourself as the architect of your mind's functions and contents, you grasp that who you are does not lie in any set of beliefs. "I am who I am by virtue of my conscious recognition of what I am not."

You are the creator and controller of your beliefs and thoughts. And with this knowledge and power, you have chosen to drop outmoded, detrimental beliefs and adopt those that are beneficial to all humankind and nature. The world has become a better place for your children and grandchildren and every generation. You have taken charge of your life and in so doing made it a little better for us all.

With God as your co-creator, you have become the master of your destiny.

"All things are possible to him who believes."
—Bible

VI
EPILOGUE

"Such as are thy habitual thoughts, such also will be the character of the mind. For the soul is dyed by the thoughts."
—Marcus Aurelius

Epilogue

"There is always hope for an individual who stops to do some serious thinking about life."
—Katherine Logan

Releasing Yourself from All Beliefs

The final thought I'd like to leave you with is the potential for releasing yourself from all beliefs. After writing a book on the enormous impact of beliefs on our lives, you may wonder how this can be.

How do we manage to continually form constructive beliefs, have an open belief system and yet let go of them?

In a world of physical form, we cannot escape from our facts, interpretations, beliefs and opinions. Nor would we want to. They form the basis for our decisions, choices and actions. It is through our beliefs that we learn about ourselves and distinguish our identity from others.

Letting go of this prodigious personal structure of reality that we've built inside our heads means to be free from its biased interference when we stand at decision points in our lives. It means being able to look anew at information and ideas and assess them from a greater depth of our being than from the infrastructure of our mind's content. It is being able to stand free from the cognitive chains of judgments and all our limiting mental constructs.

When you have built your life from a solid foundation of primary beliefs about the universe, yourself and others, paradoxically you are lifted further and further from their influence, finally standing atop the pyramid of thought form to dwell within the sphere of clear, conscious awareness.

Beliefs have been your steering wheel, to guide and direct you through life, not the real you, behind the wheel.

At last you're able to leave the confines of all beliefs and act within that powerful invisible realm of being that is forever.

APPENDIX

Mighty Belief Triads

Belief Cluster #1
Learning
❖ I believe that every effort counts in spite of the outcome.
❖ Mistakes give me feedback and accelerate the learning process.
❖ I learn from failures and move on.

Belief Cluster #2
Setbacks
❖ I know that setbacks are temporary.
❖ Setbacks make me stronger.
❖ Setbacks are simply stepping stones to my ultimate success.

Belief Cluster #3
Mind Power
❖ I have the power to direct my mind's activities.
❖ I have the power to decide what thoughts to focus on.
❖ I have the power to change my mental makeup.

Belief Cluster #4
Self Mastery
❖ Choosing my thoughts and beliefs gives me control over my emotions and moods.
❖ Taking charge of my thoughts and beliefs gives me mastery over my life and experiences.
❖ I know that I have within me everything it takes to achieve my dreams and desires.

Belief Cluster #5
Self-Direction
❖ My destiny depends on me.
❖ I act and correct as I go along.
❖ I am in charge of my life and success.

Belief Cluster #6
Others
❖ I refuse to let others discourage me from my desires and dreams.
❖ Other people can provide important feedback, however, I am the person in control of my fate.
❖ If it's to be, it's up to me.

Belief Cluster #7
Purpose
❖ I believe I have a purpose in life.
❖ My purpose is important.
❖ I am fulfilling my purpose.

Belief Cluster #8
Vision
❖ I believe in my capabilities to achieve success.
❖ I will do whatever it takes to achieve success.
❖ I deserve all the rewards of my vision of success.

Belief Cluster #9
Courage
❖ I believe that it is important to act in the face of fear.
❖ I can handle whatever situations come my way.
❖ It is okay to make mistakes and not be perfect in every way or in every situation.

Belief Cluster #10
Perseverance
❖ I believe persistence pays off.
❖ I know it is important to continue toward my dreams no matter what curves life throws me.
❖ My life is changing for the better.

Belief Cluster #11
Passion
❖ I believe what I'm doing matters and therefore fan the flames of desire for my dreams.
❖ I am excited about the challenge of overcoming obstacles to reach my goals.
❖ My efforts will pay off big.

BIBLIOGRAPHY

Resource Directory

Abe, Shigeru. The Cosmic Life of Mankind. Tokyo: Miyabi Shobo, 1986.

Anderson, Walter Truett. Reality Isn't What It Used To Be. San Francisco: Harper & Row, 1990.

Barker, Raymond Charles. Treat Yourself to Life. New York: Perigee Books, 1991.

Bohm, David. Thought as a System. London: Routledge, 1992.

Branden, Nathaniel. The Pillars of Self-Esteem, New York: Bantam Books, 1994.

Ibid. The Psychology of Self-Esteem. New York: Bantam, 1981.

Bristol, Claude M. The Magic of Believing. New York: Prentice Hall, 1985.

Brown, Les. Live Your Dreams. New York: William Morrow, 1992.

Burns, David D., M.D. Ten Days to Self-Esteem. New York: William Morrow, 1993.

Butler, Gillian Ph.D.; Hope, Tony, M.D. Managing Your Mind. New York: Oxford University Press, 1995.

Canfield, Jack; Hansen, Mark Victor. The Aladdin Factor. New York: Berkley Books, 1995.

Ibid. Chicken Soup for the Soul. Deerfield Beach, FL: Health Communications, 1996.

Ibid. Dare to Win. New York: Berkeley Books, 1996.

Capra, Fritjof. The Tao of Physics. Boston: Shambhala Publications, 1991.

Ibid. The Turning Point. New York: Bantam Books, 1982.

Carlson, Richard, Ph.D. Don't Sweat the Small Stuff... New York: Hyperion, 1997.

Carter-Scott, Cherie. If Life Is a Game, These Are the Rules: Ten Rules for Being Human, As Introduced in Chicken Soup for the Soul. Broadway Books, 1998.

Casteneda, Carlos. A Separate Reality. New York: Washington Square Press, 1972.

Chopra, Deepak, M.D. Ageless Body, Timeless Mind. New York: Harmony Books, 1993.

Clark, Glenn. The Man Who Tapped The Secrets of the Universe. Swannanoa, VA: The University of Science and Philosophy, 1989.

Cohen, Alan. Dare to be Yourself. New York: Ballantine Books, 1991.

Covey, Stephen R. First Things First. New York: Simon & Schuster, 1994.

Cypert, Samuel A. Believe & Achieve (W. Clement Stone: 17 Principles of Success). New York: Avon, 1991.

Dahl, Lynda Madden. Beyond the Winning Streak. Eugene, OR: WindSong Publishing, 1992.

Dass, Ram. Be Here Now. New York: Crown Publishing, 1971.

Dilts, Robert. Beliefs, Pathways to Health & Well-Being. Portland, OR: Metamorphous Press, 1990.

Dossey, Larry M.D. Recovering the Soul, A Scientific and Spiritual Search. New York: Bantam, 1989.

Dyer, Dr. Wayne W. Everyday Wisdom. Carson, CA.: Hay House, 1993.

Ibid. Your Sacred Self. New York: Harper-Collins, 1995.

Ibid. You'll See It When You Believe It. New York: Avon, 1990.

Ibid. Real Magic. New York: Harper, 1992.

Espposito, Henry M. Beyond Positive Thinking: Core Beliefs and Identity. Success Consultant, 1992.

Finley, Guy. Designing Your Own Destiny. St. Paul, MN: Llewellyn, 1995.

Fox, Emmet. Power Through Constructive Thinking. New York: Harper & Row, 1989.

Garfield, Charles A. Peak Performance. New York: Warner, 1985.

Gershon, David; Straub, Gail. Empowerment. New York: Dell Publishing, 1989.

Gibbs, Terri A.; Schuller, Robert Harold. Pearls of Power: For Possibility Thinkers. Word Books, 1997.

Grudin, Robert. Time and the Art of Living. New York: Harper & Row, 1982.

Hall, Lindsey; Cohn, Leigh. Self-Esteem. Carlsbad, CA: Gurze Books, 1991.

Harman, Willis, Ph.D. Global Mind Change. New York: Warner Books, 1988.

Harrison, Allen F.; Bramson, Robert M. Ph.D. The Art of Thinking. New York: Berkeley Books, 1984.

Hauck, Paul A. How to Get the Most Out of Life. Great Britain: Sheldon Press, 1988.

Helmstetter, Shad Ph.D. What To Say When You Talk To Your Self. New York: Simon & Schuster, 1986.

Ibid. Choices. New York: Simon & Schuster, 1989.

Holmes, Dr. Fenwicke Lindsay. The Law of Mind in Action. Santa Monica, CA: IBS Press, 1989.

Huxley, Aldous. The Doors of Perception. New York: Perennial Library, 1954.

Ibid. The Perennial Philosophy. New York: Perennial Library, 1944.

James, William. The Varieties of Religious Experience. New York: Collier, 1961.

Jampolsky, Gerald G. M.D. One Person Can Make A Difference. New York: Bantam, 1992.

Jampolsky, Lee Ph.D. The Art of Trust. Berkeley, CA: Celestial Arts, 1994.

Jolley, William. It Only Takes a Minute to Change Your Life. New York: St. Martins Press, 1997.

Knaus, Dr. William J. Change Your Life Now. New York: Wiley & Sons, 1994.

Krishnamurti, J. The Flight of the Eagle. New York: Harper & Row, 1972.

Loye, David. The Sphinx and the Rainbow. London: Shambhala, 1983.

Maltz, Maxwell, M.D. The Magic Power of Self Image Psychology. New York: Reward Books, 1971.

Mayer, Jeffrey J. Success Is a Journey: 7 Steps to Achieving Success in the Business of Life. New York: McGraw-Hill, 1999.

McKay, Matthew, Ph.D.; Fanning, Patrick. Prisoners of Belief. Oakland, CA: New Harbinger Publications, 1995.

McGraw, Phillip C. & McGraw, Philip. Life Strategies; Doing What Works, Doing What Matters. New York: Hyperion Books, 1999.

Oslie, Pamala. Make Your Dreams Come True: Simple Steps for Changing the Beliefs that Limit You. Amber-Allen Pub., 1998.

Patterson, Ella. 1001 Reasons to Think Positive: Special Insights to Achieve a Better Attitude Toward Life. New York: Fireside, 1997.

Paulson, Pat A.; Brown, Sharon C.; Wolf, Jo Ann. Living on Purpose. New York: Simon & Schuster, 1988.

Payutto, Bhikkhu P. A. Toward Sustainable Science. Bangkok, Thailand: Buddhadhamma Foundation, 1993.

Price, John Randolph. Practical Spirituality. Boerne, TX: Quartus Books, 1985.

Prophet, Mark L. Understanding Yourself. Malibu, CA: Summit University Press, 1985.

Roger, John; McWilliams, Peter. You Can't Afford the Luxury of a Negative Thought. Los Angeles: Prelude Press, 1989.

Ibid. Wealth 101. Los Angeles: Prelude Press, 1992.

Schuller, Robert Harold. Be Happy Attitudes. Word Books, 1997.

Ibid. If It's Going to Be, It's Up to Me: The Eight Principles of Possibility Thinking. New York: Harper Mass Market Paperbacks, 1998.

Ibid. You Can Become the Person You Want to Be. Jove Publications, 1995.

Schwartz, Tony. What Really Matters. New York: Bantam, 1995.

Simon, Sidney B.; Howe, Leland W. (Contributor), Kirschenbaum, Howard. Values Clarification/the Classic Guide to Discovering Your Truest Feelings, Beliefs, and Goals: The Classic Guide to Discovering Your Truest feelings. New York: Warner Books, 1995.

Toward A State Of Esteem. Sacramento, CA: California Task Force, 1990.

Trine, Ralph Waldo. In Tune With The Infinite. New York: Macmillan, 1970.

Tulku, Tarthang. Time, Space, and Knowledge. Emeryville, CA: Dharma Press, 1977.

von Oech, Roger. A Whack on the Side of the Head. New York: Warner Books, 1990.

Waitley, Denis. Empires of the Mind. New York: William Morrow, 1995.

Whelan, Richard. Self-Reliance, The Wisdom of Ralph Waldo Emerson. New York: Crown Publishing, 1991.

Wieder, Marcia. Making Your Dreams Come True. New York: Mastermedia Limited, 1993.

Wilber, Ken. No Boundary. London: Shambhala, 1985.

Witting, Chris J.; Witting Christian J. 21-Day Countdown to Success: Take Charge of Your Life in Less Than a Month. Career Press, 1998.

Zimmerman, Bill. Make Beliefs. New York: Bantam Books, 1992.

Zimmerman, John Sr.; Tregoe, Benjamin (Contributor) The Culture Of Success: Building A Sustained Competitive Advantage By Living Your Corporate Beliefs. New York: McGraw-Hill, 1997.

Zukav, Gary. The Seat of the Soul. New York: Simon & Schuster, 1989.

Ibid. The Dancing Wu Li Masters. New York: William Morrow, 1979.

Books on Beliefs & Reality

Anderson, Walter Truett. Reality Isn't What It Used To Be. San Francisco: Harper & Row, 1990.

Barclay, D. Believe in Yourself. New York: C.R. Gibson, 1989.

Bristol, Claude M. The Magic of Believing. New York: Prentice Hall, 1985.

Brunton, Paul. Perspectives. Burdett, NY: Larson Publications, 1987.

Cypert, Samuel. Believe & Achieve. (W. Clement Stone's 17 Principles of Success). New York: Avon, 1994.

Dahl, Lynda Madden. Beyond the Winning Streak. Eugene, OR: WindSong Publishing, 1992.

Dilts, Robert. Beliefs, Pathways to Health & Well-Being. Portland, OR: Metamorphous Press, 1990.

Dossey, Larry M.D. Recovering the Soul, A Scientific and Spiritual Search. New York: Bantam, 1989.

Dyer, Dr. Wayne W. You'll See It When You Believe It. New York: Avon Books, 1990.

Fisichella, Anthony J. Metaphysics: The Science of Life. St. Paul, MN: Llewellyn Publications, 1985.

Gershon, David; Straub, Gail. Empowerment. New York: Dell Publishing, 1989.

Glenn, Jerome Clayton. Future Mind: Artificial Intelligence. Washington, D.C.: Acropolis Books, 1989.

Goley, Elaine. Believing in Yourself. New York: Routice Corp., 1989.

Harman, Willis, Ph.D. Global Mind Change. New York: Warner Books, 1988.

Hauck, Paul A. How to Get the Most Out of Life. Great Britain: Sheldon Press, 1988.

Holmes, Dr. Fenwicke Lindsay. The Law of Mind in Action. Santa Monica, CA: IBS Press, 1989.

Huxley, Aldous. The Doors of Perception. New York: Perennial Library, 1954.

Krishnamurti, J. The Flight of the Eagle. New York: Harper & Row, 1972.

Larsen, E. et al. Believing in Myself. (Daily Meditations for Healing & Building Self-Esteem). New York: Simon & Schuster, 1991.

Pearson, E. Norman. Space, Time and Self. Wheaton, IL: Quest Books, 1990.

Russell, Peter. The Global Brain Awakens. Palo Alto, CA: Global Brain, 1995.

Smith, Huston. Beyond The Post-Modern Mind. Wheaton, IL: Quest Books, 1989.

Zimmerman, Bill. Make Beliefs. New York: Bantam Books, 1992.

For information on training programs, consultations or books and tapes, please contact:

Jan Gault International©
P.O. Box 75315
Eaton Square
Honolulu, Hawaii 96836
Telephone/Fax 800-851-6114
Email: uptime@drjan.net
Web site: http://www.drjan.net

Author Profile
Jan L. Gault Ph.D.

Jan Gault is a social psychologist, author, educator, and recognized speaker and leader in her field. She holds a Master of Science Degree in Educational Psychology and a doctorate in Social Psychology. Jan is the founder and former director of Uptime Enterprises, a San Francisco-based firm specializing in creative and personal time management. Dr. Jan has presented seminars and taught at numerous universities, including University of Hawaii, Central Texas College and Hawaii Pacific University.

Jan Gault is the author of many articles and books including *Free Time—Making your Leisure Count* (Wiley & Sons) and *Play & Grow Rich*, a motivational book for entrepreneurs. Jan has also authored and narrated a number of motivational and inspirational audio and video products. These include *"Success Principles & Beliefs," "25 Ways to Build Self Esteem," "Perseverance & Passion,"* and *"Strategies for Success."*

Jan's programs, seminars and lectures have been presented to a wide range of audiences, and through a variety of business and professional organizations including American Medical Association, San Francisco Business League, National Soft Drink Bottlers Assn., American Management Association, and the United States Military Joint Intelligence Agency. Jan has received international publicity and acclaim for her presentations, books and consultations. She has been featured on over 200 radio and television networks and media throughout the United States and Canada.

Jan's articles, book excerpts and interviews have been published in *Glamour Magazine, San Francisco Business Journal, Money Magazine, Christian Science Monitor, San Jose Mercury News, Bottom Line Personal, The Melbourne Age,* and *The Journal of Leisure Research.*

Dr. Jan currently lives in Hawaii where she has a private practice specializing in creative time empowerment and successful living.

NOTES

Printed in the United States
4832

9 780923 699253